The Real Estate Wealth Creator Blueprint

Keys to overcoming fear, lack of money, and inexperience, to possess the land!

Dexter B. Jenkins

Contents

ENDORSEMENTS

The Real Estate Wealth Creator Blueprint by Dexter B. Jenkins isn't your typical feel-good faith and finance book. It's a wake-up call, plain and simple. For far too long, many believers have been trapped by misguided notions that faith and wealth don't mix, or worse, that seeking financial success is somehow 'unholy.' Dexter blows that myth out of the water. As a pastor and financial mentor, he challenges you to stop limiting God's abundance with a middle-class mindset. Real estate is the tool, but your faith is the engine that drives wealth creation. This book forces you to confront your beliefs about money, faith, and God's will — and if you're not ready for that, this book isn't for you. But if you're tired of playing small and are ready to align your beliefs with action, The Real Estate Wealth Creator Blueprint is the no-nonsense guide that will take you there.

Kadena Tate

Revenue Strategist and Business Model Designer

CEO, 50 Shades of Paid Intl LLC

www.KadenaTate.com

In The Real Estate Wealth Creator Blueprint, Dexter B. Jenkins brings his decades of financial expertise, leadership, and faith-based insights to the forefront, offering readers a comprehensive guide to overcoming financial barriers and building generational wealth. With clarity and conviction, Dexter Jenkins addresses the common fears and misconceptions about real estate investing, showing that success is not reserved for a select few but is attainable for all, making every reader feel included and valued.

Dexter's unique approach, rooted in his personal faith and financial stewardship, makes this book a must-read for anyone serious about transforming their economic life. His use of real-world examples and practical strategies demystifies the complexities of real estate and wealth creation. Dexter's deep belief in the power of faith combined with sound financial principles shines through every page, empowering readers to take control of their financial future.

Jenkins's ability to speak directly to individuals who may feel marginalized in finance, particularly communities of color, sets him apart. His message is clear: with the right mindset, mentorship, and practical steps, anyone can achieve financial freedom and begin to possess the land.

Jenkins's SHIP Method (Stewardship, Ownership, and Entrepreneurship) lays out a step-by-step plan to help readers reframe their relationship with money, eliminate limiting beliefs, and create a sustainable plan for long-term wealth. Whether you're new to real estate or a seasoned investor, this book offers actionable insights that will inspire you to embrace real estate as a critical tool for financial empowerment. Dexter B. Jenkins' blend of faith and finance gives readers the confidence and tools to dream about building wealth and making it a reality. The Real Estate Wealth Creator Blueprint is the perfect guide for those who feel overwhelmed by the challenges of limited resources, lack of experience, or fear of the unknown.

Dr. David M. Walker

Author, The Champion's Mind: How to Defeat Giants and Win

www.DrWalkerSpeaks.com

Pastor Dexter B. Jenkins' "The Real Estate Wealth Creator Blueprint" stands as a comprehensive and deeply insightful roadmap for those seeking not only financial success but also alignment with spiritual principles. As an entrepreneur with over 25 years in the real estate industry, I have learned that true wealth creation is built on much more than just strategies and numbers. Jenkins brilliantly demonstrates how real estate serves as a powerful tool for leverage and long-term wealth, but he also emphasizes the critical need to break free from the limiting middle-class mindset that often holds us back from achieving financial exceptionalism. What makes this book truly resonate with me is how it intertwines faith with financial pursuits. Throughout my journey, I've learned to lean not on my own understanding but trust in divine guidance. Jenkins echoes this principle, reminding readers that faith plays a central role in any wealth-building endeavor. His teachings underscore the importance of ensuring that what we believe is congruent with how we think — only then can we fully unlock the potential for creating real, lasting wealth. In my experience, the most successful ventures arise from aligning our spiritual convictions with practical actions, and Pastor Jenkins' blueprint is a powerful resources for doing just that. Whether you're just beginning your real estate journey or looking to elevate your existing strategy, this book is a must-read for integrating faith, purpose, and financial success.

LaRick Calhoun

Instagram @larickcalhoun | LinkedIn @larickcalhoun

www.LarickCalhoun.com

Hi, my name is Tommy Jones, and if you're looking for a book that will not only change your life but rewrite your destiny, you owe it to yourself to add this one to your library. My good friend, Pastor Dexter Jenkins, has written his new best-seller, The Real Estate Wealth Creator Blueprint.

Listen: if you've ever wanted to get into a position where you're paid what you're worth, real estate is definitely the vehicle. You'll learn how to find properties, use a proven system to create a blueprint for wealth, and, most importantly, how to build a legacy for your family.

The Bible says a wise man stores up an inheritance for his children's children. If you're wise, you owe it to yourself to read Dexter Jenkins' The Real Estate Wealth Creator Blueprint. You can thank me later.

Tommy Jones

Wealth Through Real Estate

www.WTREonline.com

As someone who has spent over 20 years in the real estate industry, completing over 40 projects and funding over $100 million in hard money loans, I've learned that success in this field requires more than just knowledge of the market — it requires the right mindset, financial literacy, and unwavering faith. Dexter Jenkins masterfully addresses these key pillars in The Real Estate Wealth Creator Blueprint. His practical insights on leveraging real estate for wealth creation, combined with the vital role of faith and financial intelligence, provide a roadmap for overcoming fear and inexperience.

This book is a powerful guide for both aspiring and seasoned investors who seek to build wealth, not only in assets but in mindset. Dexter's approach to breaking the middle-class mindset and striving for financial exceptionalism resonates deeply with the principles I've applied in my own career. Whether you're new to real estate or a seasoned investor, The Real Estate Wealth Creator Blueprint will challenge you to elevate your thinking and take decisive action toward financial freedom.

Dexter's clear, faith-centered approach makes this book a must-read for anyone serious about real estate investing. I highly recommend it.

Robert Nichols

Real Estate Entrepreneur and Hard Money Lender

Author of How To Flip Your Way To Freedom

www.MIGXM.com

Pastor Dexter B. Jenkins is a faith-based financial mentor, and a popular guest on my Money Making Conversations Master Class podcast, because of his background as a renowned real estate investor and financial expert. He has with more than two decades of experience in the financial services industry. During my podcast interview with Pastor Jenkins, I discovered how passionate he is about helping families build generational wealth with easy-to-implement steps. His book "The Real Estate Wealth Creator Blueprint" isn't your typical feel-good faith book, because it provides a plan of action with step-by-step instructions. He demonstrates in great detail how real estate can serve as a powerful tool to leverage long-term wealth. The dream of achieving a consistent home in the middle class ranks is only one property purchase away and it starts with "The Real Estate Wealth Creator Blueprint."

Rushion McDonald

Host of Money Making Conversations Master Class

Foreword

LaShawne Holland

I first met Dexter B. Jenkins several years ago, just after I released my first book. It was during a time when I was eager to get my message out to as many people as possible, and I did so through various channels, including podcast interviews. After one of those interviews, I received an email that stopped me in my tracks. Dexter had heard the podcast, and he reached out with a few insightful questions. But it wasn't just the questions that caught my attention — it was his next statement. He said he wanted to purchase 100 copies of my book for the members of his congregation. That single act spoke volumes to me.

Very few pastors are willing to invest in their people the way Dexter does. To him, this is not about building wealth for wealth's sake. What he teaches isn't a hobby or a sideline; it's a way of being — a lifestyle that he embodies every single day. Dexter Jenkins has a heart of gold, and his mission is simple yet powerful: he wants everyone to walk in their God-given right to abundance. Because abundance is your birthright. And it's a birthright that's accessible when you understand how to create and seize opportunities — especially in real estate.

What sets Dexter apart is not just his passion for real estate but his depth of knowledge. His understanding doesn't come from barbershop conversations or late-night infomercials promising instant riches. Dexter was raised in this world — his father was a real estate investor. The principles of property, investment, and generational wealth are in his blood. He has lived them, learned from them, and mastered them. But his education didn't stop there. He also comes from the world of investment banking, a realm that armed him with strategies and tools that few others possess. Dexter understands the intricacies of capital, the mechanics of leverage, and the art of deal-making. This combination of expertise positions him uniquely to help you navigate the complexities of real estate and secure a future that advances not just your personal goals but the Kingdom of God.

The beauty of real estate is that it's not a field reserved for the elite. You don't need a specific background or pedigree to get started; you just need the right mindset, the right strategies, and the right guidance. The strategies Dexter outlines in this book are needful because they give you the advantage in life. They allow you to break free from the limitations that may have held back previous generations, and they empower you to create wealth that changes your family's destiny.

If there's one truth I've learned over the years, it's this: Opportunities find you in motion, not standing still. Dexter embodies this principle. He understands that to create your own opportunities, you need to be willing to take action, move forward, and keep learning. This book is not just a collection of strategies — it's a roadmap for those who are ready to do the work, for those who are willing to take action and change the trajectory of their lives.

Dexter's passion for real estate is rooted in something deeper than profit margins. It's about advancing the Kingdom of God. It's about empowering individuals to live out their full potential and build a legacy that stretches beyond their own lives. The Real Estate Wealth Creator Blueprint is not just a guide; it's a call to action. It's a reminder that abundance is not a distant dream but a divine right, waiting to be claimed by those who are willing to step up and do the work.

So, as you turn these pages, prepare to be inspired. Prepare to be challenged. But most importantly, prepare to be equipped. Dexter B. Jenkins is here to show you that real estate isn't just an investment. It's a lifestyle, a calling, and a pathway to true, sustainable abundance.

Here's to your journey, and here's to building a legacy that honors God and secures your family's future for generations to come.

LaShawne Holland

Wealth Coach & Best-Selling Author

LaShawne Holland
Founder, Holland & Holland Enterprises, LLC
www.lashawneholland.com
FREE BOOK www.borntomultiplybook.com
P.O. Box 1242, Brandywine, MD 20613
301.579.6586

Acknowledgements

I would like to thank my wife Kendra Jenkins for all the love and support and her willingness to do life with me. Whether in ministry or in business, your unwavering belief in me and what we could accomplish together has been invaluable.

To my children Danielle, Cameron, and Sydney, thank you for giving me the title of Dad/Pop and making our house one full of fun and laughter.

To Bishop Gideon Thompson, my spiritual father and a man whose biblical teachings and, more importantly, real-life example has helped to transform me into the man I am today.

And of course, my parents, Samuel and Annie Jenkins. They birthed me into a loving home and taught me the principles of loving God, along with business, finance, and real estate.

Introduction

Why Building Wealth Is Mandatory and How Real Estate Can Help Get You There

Building wealth is no longer optional but mandatory!

As a pastor, real estate developer, author, and podcaster, I have spent the last 3 decades at the intersection of faith, business, and finance. It is quite exciting living within this dynamic trifecta!

People often ask, why is someone who is a pastor so involved in real estate and in the financial world? My answer is always the same.

It is through our faith that we achieve success in God's spiritual realm, and through our knowledge of tangible assets such as real estate, that we achieve success in His natural material world.

I am of the personal belief that everyone must decide to become wealthy! Most people in our society are very casual when it comes to wealth creation and accumulation. They've fallen into the trap that middle-class living is okay. It's not! When you're in the middle, your financial well-being is always controlled by other people's performance and decisions. *Being in the middle of anything is not a place of success. At best it is a place of mediocrity.*

Art Williams, who was an insurance tycoon with A.L. Williams Insurance Company, used to say that being in the middle was being average and ordinary. And he would follow that statement with, "Call me anything but average and ordinary."

Recent events such as pandemics, hyperinflation, and changing political climates have shown us that with middle-class living, you are always only one mistake or one poor decision away from poverty. In order to ensure your success and establish generational wealth for your children, you must decide to be exceptional in your wealth accumulation.

Now we must answer the pressing question.

Why don't more of us make the decision to aggressively go after wealth?

I believe the simple answer is that we have been incorrectly programmed and conditioned.

The Poverty Quadrant

Whether speaking on stages to many or one-on-one with individuals, I always introduce this concept called the Poverty Quadrant (PQ).

The Poverty Quadrant deals with the inner game of wealth by examining the spiritual, cultural, environmental, and financial programming we have received and how that impacts our beliefs and subsequently our financial behaviors. You'll learn more about this in the next chapter, but just understand this for now: Your wealth (or poverty) is directly related to the spiritual, environmental, cultural, and financial conditioning you received from your parents, your schools, your city, and yes, even your pastor.

Breaking the Mold

Make no mistake. The decision to become wealthy is an act of courage that many people simply will never make. You are going to have to fight your own internal demons as well as the external pressure of friends and family who have settled for the status quo.

Before I continue, I think it's important that I define wealth. Robert Kiyosaki has a great way of defining wealth. He describes wealth as the amount of time you can live without working. For example, if you have $20,000 saved up and your monthly expenses are $4,000, you are five months wealthy. You can see how this definition moves the target from money to time. Understand this:

Wealth is more time dependent than money dependent!

I like Mr. Kiyosaki's definition, but I like my Grandma Catherine's definition of wealth as well.

Grandma Catherine was a snowbird. She enjoyed balancing her winters in the southern states and the summer months in the north. On one of her visits to the north, I found myself sitting in one of my aunt's living rooms enjoying family. I don't remember much of the conversation, but something stood out to me, and it still sticks with me today. In the middle of the conversation, she stopped and looked at me to say,

"Dexter, I am a wealthy woman."

I nodded my head slowly, but I was internally questioning what she said. She never drove a fancy car, wore overly expensive clothes and I knew she didn't throw around money. I was puzzled — but now I understand what she was saying.

She had 10 children and tons of grandchildren to delight in. She had no need to work and had more than enough money to travel across the USA visiting her family and creating memories. She had freedom. And that's how I view wealth. Combining Robert Kiyosaki's mentality with my wealthy grandmother's sagely statement.

For me, wealth is this:

Wealth is having what you need when you need it.

Real estate without a doubt has the power to create a lifestyle that makes sure you have what you need when you need it. This is why I believe that over 90% of millionaires attribute their wealth to some form of involvement in real estate. When you determine how much money you need to live your desired life, it's very easy to structure a plan to actively or passively reach that number with real estate.

That's how I saw my parents build their wealth, that's how I saw most of the richest people I know build their wealth, and it's how my wife and I are actively building our wealth.

It's also how I want to teach you to build your wealth.

In the following pages, I will explain the basics of real estate, and share some of my wins (and losses) with one goal in mind: to help you become what I call a Real Estate Wealth Creator.

A Real Estate Wealth Creator is defined as someone who has:

1. **Decided they are going to become wealthy**
2. **Decided that real estate is going to be either the or a primary tool used in achieving that goal**

Let's get started!

1

Cultivating the Right Mindset for Wealth Creation

In this chapter, we are going to begin cultivating the right mindset for wealth creation. The quote below by Joe Ensor, one of my first sales mentors, indicates why we have to do this vital work.

"Success is a language, and for most folks, it is a foreign language."

The wisdom in these words has only deepened with time, revealing layers of truth about the nature of success and the barriers that many face in achieving it. Joe's observation speaks to a fundamental reality: most people spend their entire lives toiling away, yet they find themselves stuck in a cycle of financial poverty.

The fact that most people work their entire lives and at best have a mediocre retirement living off a fixed income tells you that there is something most people do not understand regarding money and wealth building. The dogma we were fed about going to school, getting good grades, pursuing some sort of higher education, and working hard is a played-out manual for success. Honestly, I do not know if it ever worked, but because that was all we heard we took it as gospel truth.

In reality the truth is this: it's not merely about working hard. Working hard just wears you out and makes you tired. It is 100 percent about thinking differently. Our beliefs, and the way we think, about wealth, success, and our own potential, significantly influence our trajectory toward or away from prosperity. Our mind can be our greatest ally or our biggest foe while seeking financial freedom. Believe me — it's not enough to possess knowledge and skills on how to excel in real estate. We must all adopt the proper mindset to see lasting success. In this chapter, we'll discuss the necessary changes you need to make to build the perfect Real Estate Wealth Creator mindset. We are going to do that by doing a deep dive into a concept I call the Poverty Quadrant which was mentioned earlier in the book.

The Poverty Quadrant

Several years ago, I asked myself a question: Why do so few people excel financially? We live in a time when you can access all types of financial information and money advice with a few clicks of a button and yet, most people are still broke. Let me insert a quick reality check here. Becoming wealthy is not only about information; it is more about the mental transformation one has to go through in order to take advantage of the information. In chapter 7 we will be going into implementation mode in order to take advantage of what you are learning in this book.

After weeks of thinking on and around the subject, the Poverty Quadrant was birthed. The PQ as I like to call it, has really shaped how I think about the subject of personal finance and wealth building. I call it my tool to help you examine the inner game of wealth building. Most mistakenly think that their ability to make money is controlled by outside forces such as their boss, who is in the White House, and other external factors. In reality whether we end up in wealth or poverty is almost always dictated by our beliefs, thoughts, and actions which are all internally driven. Our beliefs, thoughts, and attitudes are a by-product of where and how you grew up, the schools you attended, the churches you were a part of, and the list could go on and on. In order to break out of the poverty quadrant we must begin to question the validity of the messages we heard while in those environments.

The Spiritual Quadrant

As you can see from the diagram, all of the main factors affecting your ability to create wealth can be broken into four main categories: Spiritual, Environmental, Cultural, and Financial. Let's start with the Spiritual Quadrant.

Years ago, when I was selling life insurance and investments, I had an appointment with a young woman. Our discussion was centered around her future saving goals, preparing for retirement, and college savings for her daughter. However, very early on in the conversation, I knew we wouldn't be a good fit. She was an extremely bright young lady, but it was very clear that she believed creating lasting, generational wealth went against some of her core spiritual beliefs. Essentially what she told me was this, "I do not care anything about money or this world's riches, I just want to go to heaven."

To support her stance, she gave several scriptural references stressing the importance of heaven and being pleasing to God, while downplaying the importance of our earthly journey and the material things we need to support that journey.

Just like that young lady, many struggle with the subject because of the programming we have received from our churches. Our belief system and our mindsets have been contaminated through misquoted verses such as money being the root of all evil found in 1 Timothy 6:10.

"For the love of money is the root of all kinds of evils. It is through this craving that some have wandered away from the faith and pierced themselves with many pangs."

I want you to notice that the verse actually states that the love of money is the root of all evil. God desires us to love Him, people, and ourselves, not money. See Matthew 22:37-39 to reference what I just said. If you love anything else other than the three things mentioned in those verses. You have entered into a perverted love relationship which is a dangerous relationship to be in.

Another misunderstood verse is found in Matthew 19:24.

"Again, I tell you, it is easier for a camel to go through the eye of a needle than for someone who is rich to enter the kingdom of God."

Jesus was not glorifying being poor. He was speaking about some rich people having difficulty shifting their trust from their money and onto God. I just gave you the CliffsNotes on those two verses for the sake of providing some understanding. But you can see how people get duped into believing that poverty is piety and that wealth is wicked.

In order to break free from the bondage of the Spiritual Quadrant, one must become certain about what the Bible teaches about money, finance, and business. The books of Proverbs and Ecclesiastes are great places to start. These two books are full of sound financial and business wisdom and were written by King Solomon. It is reported that King Solomon was the richest man to ever have lived. In addition to the Bible, it is a good practice to read other business and finance books, attend seminars, and even use YouTube. All of the above will help to build a solid financial foundation and empower you to break free from the shackles found within the Spiritual Quadrant.

The Environmental Quadrant

Closely tied to the Spiritual Quadrant's influence is the second quadrant — the Environmental Quadrant. Phrases like "People like us have to work hard for our money" and "Do you think money grows on trees?" reflect a worldview where financial struggle is normalized, and wealth is seen as unattainable or the result of extraordinary effort. Recognizing environmental messages that influence our financial beliefs and behaviors is crucial for personal growth and financial well-being.

By questioning our thinking and isolating destructive environmental messages, individuals can begin to challenge limiting beliefs, reframe their relationship with money, and pursue financial health and prosperity. This process not only fosters a healthier financial mindset but also allows for an individual to break out of the Environmental Quadrant if they are not where they desire to be financially.

Without a doubt, I can speak to the power of being in the right environments. The way I think about business, finance, and real estate has been shaped by the environments I have been fortunate enough to be exposed to. Later in the book, I am going to share about when my wife and I were buying our first home. I believed it was normal to own a multi-family home, which had not been my wife's experience. The purchase of that first 3-family house in Dorchester, Massachusetts, put us on the path to becoming Real Estate Wealth Creators.

The Cultural Quadrant

Next let's touch on the Cultural Quadrant. This quadrant in particular has the power to relegate people to bench warmer status when it comes to the game of wealth creation. In this quadrant there are common beliefs, thoughts, and words that are controlling the masses. When you hear people using limiting language around wealth creation and financial success, you have just stepped over into the Cultural Quadrant. When these messages are heard, internalized, and believed, individuals often are discouraged from exploring viable paths for achieving financial success. I have listed a few common messages below.

"Wealth is for athletes, entertainers, and rappers."

This message suggests that only a few high-profile professions can lead to one having significant wealth. If you are not Michael Jordan, Lebron James, Tiger Woods, Taylor Swift, or Snoop Dogg, wealth and financial good fortune are forever out of your reach. This can discourage individuals from exploring other viable paths to financial success. For instance, entrepreneurs, investors, and professionals in various fields like technology, healthcare, and business also amass substantial wealth. In fact, they often are able to amass much more wealth than of the occupations listed above. By believing that wealth is only achievable through celebrity status, many may overlook the importance of innovation, entrepreneurship, and skill development in other areas.

"Rich people are crooks and greedy."

This stereotype can create a negative association with wealth, implying that unethical behavior is a prerequisite for financial success. Such a belief can discourage honest and ethical conduct in business or personal finances, as people might think that playing by the rules won't lead them to wealth. Moreover, it can lead to resentment and a lack of motivation to pursue wealth, thinking it may require compromising one's values.

"You need a college degree to make good money."

While education can certainly be a powerful tool for increasing earning potential, this statement is far from the truth. It ignores the financial success achieved by skilled tradespeople, self-taught individuals, and entrepreneurs without formal higher education. In today's digital age, alternative education paths, such as certifications, apprenticeships, and online courses, can also lead to lucrative careers. Believing that a traditional college degree is the only way can deter people from pursuing these viable alternatives.

Changing these culturally ingrained mindsets starts with education and awareness. It involves highlighting and valuing diverse paths to success, recognizing ethical wealth creation, and understanding the broad spectrum of opportunities available beyond the conventional narratives. By challenging these stereotypes and offering broader, more inclusive views of success, individuals can be empowered to pursue a wide range of aspirations that align with their unique skills, values, and interests.

The Financial Quadrant

The financial messages we receive in this quadrant from society, educational institutions, family, and media significantly influence our attitudes and behaviors regarding money management, career choices, and investment strategies. Here are a few common quotes that many believe without recognizing the detrimental impact it will have on their ability to produce wealth.

"Focus on getting good grades and working hard, and you will do well financially..."

I touched on this one earlier in the book and wanted to go a little deeper around this thought. Thirty maybe forty years ago, the traditional route of academic excellence and hard work was viewed as the surefire way to wealth. While a college degree certainly meant more back then, it wasn't a 100% guarantee of creating lasting wealth. While education and effort are crucial, this mindset can overlook other equally important financial skills like networking, entrepreneurship, and financial literacy. Many in our society have advanced degrees and look successful but are struggling financially.

"Go get a safe and secure job with benefits..."

Similar to the idea of a college degree, seeking a career is often viewed as the best path for achieving financial stability. This can be a great place to start and is the best place for many, but it might also discourage taking calculated risks that could lead to greater innovation and potentially higher financial rewards. Not everyone needs to start a business, but they certainly need to view options for building wealth and creating financial leverage for themselves outside of their 9-5 career. I am of the personal belief that having only one source of income is extremely dangerous. I am going to conclude this point by quoting Warren Buffet: *"If you don't find a way to make money while you sleep, you will work until you die."*

"Save your money in the bank because investing of any sort is risky..."

This cautious approach prioritizes security over growth, which is suitable in some cases but definitely misleading as a universal strategy. When it comes to money, security of any sort is a myth! While all investments consist of some risk, informed and well-planned investment strategies are essential for wealth accumulation and protection against inflation. Frankly, money just grows too slowly if left in the bank and you can never save your way to wealth. Look up the rule of 72 if you want to go deeper around the subject. By categorically labeling all investments as risky, this message discourages the development of financial literacy and the potential for higher returns through the taking of calculated risks.

"The subject of money is too hard to understand..."

Money deserves time and attention, but it doesn't have to be overly complicated to understand. The perceived barrier of financial complexity keeps too many people from engaging in building their wealth. They feel underqualified and throw their hands up in frustration. This mindset can lead to avoidance and passivity, where individuals may miss out on opportunities for wealth creation or fail to protect their financial interests effectively. Promoting financial education as a critical and essential skill is part of a multi-pronged solution to helping people master their money.

Overcoming The Poverty Quadrant

You might be asking yourself, "How do I overcome The Poverty Quadrant?" The first step to any type of change is awareness. Most often we are operating on a subconscious level when it comes to our money and wealth creation. No matter what quadrant you might have identified yourself in, the keys to breaking free of the PQ and cultivating the mindset of a Real Estate Wealth Creator can be summarized in three simple steps.

1. **Education:** The first step is to educate yourself on beliefs and behaviors that point you toward wealth creation not away from

it. Much like the woman I met with years ago, many of us need to become aware of the thoughts and attitudes that hold us back from reaching our highest financial potential.

2. **Entertainment:** Entertainment can be dangerous. Whether it's music, TV shows, or the places you hang out for fun, your entertainment choices often shape your perspective on life. If you are constantly listening to music that downplays the rich or presents certain lifestyles as the only way to wealth, you are limiting your mind with the music you listen to. Be wary of the shows you watch and the things you ingest — they could be destroying your chances of building lasting wealth.

3. **Engagement:** There's a common saying among the self-improvement community: "You are the sum of the five people you spend the most time with." In other words, the people you hang out with will determine your future. While it might sound a bit dramatic, this statement couldn't be truer. That's why the messages we mentioned above are able to seep into your mind without you even noticing, because you are constantly surrounded by them at church, school, and maybe even your home. Be sure that you are engaging with fellow wealth creators on a consistent basis, and you will become the next one.

Chapter One Takeaways

- Real Estate Wealth Creation is a direct result of cultivating the proper mindset.
- The Poverty Quadrant is a tool to help you examine the inner

game of wealth.

- Success is a language, and for most folks, it is a foreign language.

2

THE ROLE OF FAITH IN REAL ESTATE WEALTH CREATION

You don't have to look any further than Genesis 1:1-2 to see that God is into real estate and specifically the development of real estate.

"In the beginning God created the heavens and the earth. Now the earth was formless and empty, darkness was over the surface of the deep, and the Spirit of God was hovering over the waters."

Long before HGTV existed, God did a major renovation on a dark, empty, and formless earth. Interesting thought, huh? God, in my opinion, was acting as the original Real Estate Wealth Creator by taking undeveloped land and turning it into something that is valuable.

In this chapter we are going to talk about combining faith and Real Estate Wealth Creation. Most consider even the mentioning of financial things and the things of God to be taboo. But since I have lived at the intersection of faith, finance, and business for so long, it is second nature to me. I predict that for some of you this is going to be a paradigm shifting chapter. As I often say when speaking to live audiences, hold on to your wig, this is going to be good!

In August of 2023, I was fortunate enough to speak at the Power Networking Conference (PNC) hosted by Dr. George Fraser in Houston, Texas. If you are not familiar with PNC, it is probably the largest gathering of black and brown people for the sole purpose of networking to build collective financial strength and solidarity.

The room was full of real estate entrepreneurs doing some tremendous things in the real estate space, as well as others on the come-up desiring to learn the real estate game. About a week before the event, the organizer called and asked if I could specifically cover two specific things.

1. What the Bible says regarding God's desire for His people to own real estate or become Real Estate Wealth Creators.

2. How I as a pastor was successfully reconciling my real estate activities with my faith.

Most of the things I will be sharing with you in this chapter will be from that talk at PNC.

God's Desire for His People and Real Estate Wealth Creation

Owning real estate is both a biblical and Godly concept.

I know what I said is a bold statement and one that must be backed up by scripture. Just so you know, in order for something to be considered a biblical truth, you must be able to find that truth in a minimum of 2-3 places. So, with that in mind, I am going to enlist the help of King Solomon, who was reportedly the wisest and wealthiest man to ever have lived.

This Hebrew King was responsible for writing the majority of the book of Proverbs which is, in my opinion, the best book on finance, business, and money. Here are just a few examples of what the wisest and wealthiest man had to say about real estate. You will see that he put an emphasis on land ownership in order to create financial abundance.

Proverbs 12:11

"Those who work their <u>land</u> will have abundant food, but those who chase fantasies have no sense."

Proverbs 28:19

"Those who work their <u>land</u> will have abundant food, but those who chase fantasies will have their fill of poverty."

There are several other real estate related references in Proverbs, but my favorite verse is found in Proverbs 19:14.

"<u>Houses</u> and wealth are inherited from parents, but a prudent wife is from the LORD."

I really like that verse because we can see from God's word that houses and real estate should be passed down from one generation to another.

Pivoting away from King Solomon for a moment and stepping back into the (PNC), I shared with the audience a conversation I had with my great grandmother on my mother's side who lived in Alabama. I was about 11 years old when she told me how she and her husband used to make 25 cents a week pulling up tree stumps. If you have ever been in the deep south during the summer, you know how hot it can get out in those fields. I can imagine that both her and my great grandfather shed tons of blood, sweat, and tears.

The Bible talks about God remembering the blood and hearing the cries of those who were wronged and or denied justice. Check out Cain and Abel in Genesis 4:10 and field laborers in James 5:4. I am of the thought process that the blood of my great grandparents and our other ancestors is crying out to God for economic justice and that real estate investing is one of the ways we are going to collect.

Reconciling Real Estate, My Faith, and My Role

When it comes to how I successfully reconcile real estate and my faith, it goes back to my childhood roots. My mother Annie Jenkins was a woman of great faith who stressed the importance of having a relationship with God. On the other hand, I watched my dad purchase real estate and operate as a full-time barber. Mr. Eddie's Barbershop, which was the barbershop my dad first worked at before starting his own, was my first business school.

My experience has been that most people are torn regarding their faith and wealth creation. In order to have success in this business, there must be congruence between your real estate activities and your faith life. To those seeking to integrate their faith life and real estate life, I offer the following practical advice:

1. **Do Daily Devotions:** Begin each day with prayer and Scripture reading to stay connected to your faith and gain clarity for your business decisions. Pay particular attention to Proverbs and Ecclesiastes.

2. **Seek Godly Counsel:** Surround yourself with mentors and advisors who share your faith and can provide both spiritual and practical financial guidance.

3. **Maintain Integrity:** Conduct all business dealings with honesty and transparency, reflecting the values of your faith.

4. **Serve Others:** Use your real estate ventures as a platform to serve and uplift communities, aligning your business with a higher purpose.

5. **Embrace Stewardship:** Manage your resources responsibly, viewing wealth as a tool for positive impact rather than an end in itself.

6. **Stay Resilient:** Trust in God's plan, especially during challenging times, and view setbacks as opportunities for growth and learning.

Let me put on my pastor's hat for a second and speak on the subject of real estate wealth creation. When we first started our church back in 2012, I quickly saw that there was a need for my congregation to learn not only about prayer, forgiveness, and other spiritual things but to also be taught principles of financial literacy and real estate wealth creation.

In particular, there was a couple who lost their house through a foreclosure. When I found out the details of what happened. The foreclosure could have easily been prevented and the house kept within their family. I took that foreclosure personally and vowed that as long as I pastored people that I would share the knowledge I have.

I personally believe that any pastor who does not care about the spiritual, physical, relational, and financial well-being of their people is practicing pastoral abuse.

There is also a tremendous opportunity that lies before us as people of faith to practically impact our communities through both housing and job creation. When you consider the amount of housing that is needed for the less fortunate it is astounding. Often, I am in meetings where we are talking about creating housing for seniors, the homeless, returning citizens, and the list goes on and on. States and cities are stretched to the max and are looking for partners to help with the lack of quality housing for people. I am reminded of what Jesus said in Matthew 25:40:

"The King will reply, Truly I tell you, whatever you did for one of the least of these brothers and sisters of mine, you did for me."

When we act as Real Estate Wealth Creators, we can do for the least of those who Jesus is referring to in the above text.

And of course, when you create housing, you are also creating jobs for both men and women in your local community. Our real estate activities can create a ripple effect in the communities we reside in and allow us to do good as we are doing well!

Let me close this chapter with this: you must settle in your heart and in your mind that it is okay for you to become a Real Estate Wealth Creator. The Bible is replete with references to land and real estate, illustrating its importance from a spiritual and financial standpoint. Just as God wanted to take His people to a promise land many years ago, I believe His desire is still the same today. Again, owning real estate is both a biblical and Godly concept.

Chapter Two Takeaways

- God is into real estate development.
- There must be congruence between your real estate activities and your faith life.
- There is a tremendous opportunity for the faith community to practically impact the less fortunate in our communities through our Real Estate Wealth Creator activities.

3

Why You Must Raise Your Level of Financial Intelligence and Literacy

"*Financial ignorance is expensive.*" *Dexter B. Jenkins*

Though the main premise of this book is centered around you becoming a Real Estate Wealth Creator, it would be foolish of us not to talk about the importance of you raising your financial intelligence level. As I said above, financial ignorance is extremely expensive. Let me give you an example of what financial intelligence looks like in real time.

Recently, a friend of mine was discussing how to strategically bring in more money to pay for his daughter's college education by investing in large apartment complexes. His plan was simple and a great example of what I mean when I talk about someone being financially literate.

The savvy financial plan was to purchase a large apartment complex and allow the apartment complex to pay for his daughter's college education. You may be asking how is that possible? Well, by rounding up 200 or so investors, alongside with some bank financing to purchase the asset, he could then have the tenants pay back both the investors and the bank. This would allow him to have zero dollars out of pocket and still have the distinction of being the proud father of a college graduate. Instead of using his own dollars to pay for college tuition, he was using both financial intelligence and financial literacy to help his daughter get through school.

One of the things that financially literate and intelligent people always look to do is to transfer the cost of things to others. This allows their dollars to be continually at work in their assets and other investments. More on that later.

You may be asking, what is your definition of financial intelligence and financial literacy? I define financial intelligence and financial literacy as the ability to understand a few basic financial concepts and then make wise decisions that will benefit you financially.

Looking a little closer at the definition, understand that financial literacy means having the ability to understand and grasp, while intelligence speaks to having the ability to make choices. When you are able to put those two components together, you are cooking with financial grease. My friend understood how to read his daughter's situation and then choose a financial plan based on the knowledge he accumulated over time in the areas of money, debt, and real estate.

As I mentioned earlier, I spent over two decades in the financial services industry selling life insurance and mutual funds. And have read countless books on the subject of personal finance, wealth building, and real estate. If you do not believe me, ask my wife as she is always trying to get me to downsize my book collection.

My overall philosophy around financial literacy, financial intelligence, and real estate wealth creation is summed up in something I refer to as The SHIP Method. The idea is simple. If you want to improve your finances, you can do so by mastering: Stewardship, Ownership, and Entrepreneurship. If you want a copy of The SHIP Method, go to DexterBJenkins.com to download a copy. We will only be glancing briefly at this method in this chapter.

Through the study and application of The Ship Method, I came up with 8 characteristics of people who I would define as being financially literate and financial intelligent people. Depending on how you categorize the 8 characteristics, you will find that they are woven all throughout Stewardship, Ownership, and Entrepreneurship.

So, here we go, financially literate and financially intelligent individuals:

1. Know How to Create a Spending Plan

A spending plan is the first step to successfully stewarding your money. Let me say this before we get into the nuts and bolts of this section. A spending plan will not make you wealthy. Though a spending plan is critical to your financial success, and provides needed structure, spending plans alone do not produce wealth. The line below sums up my thoughts on the subject.

Spending plans are all about you telling your money what to do!

Money must be given specific direction and instructions. We all know from experience, that if we don't direct our money, it quickly slips away. When speaking on this subject. I often give the example of when in days of old we had to physically cash our checks at a bank. If you were not careful, your money was frivolously spent if it was not told what to do.

If we are going to give our money direction and instruction, what should the breakdown ideally be? I teach aiming for either a 10/10/80 or 10/20/70 allocation. This means that when your income comes in, you should tithe 10% to your church or favorite charity, allocate 10% to your investments, and live on 80% for all your other expenses. Depending on your starting point, you might not begin with those allocations, but this gives you something to aim for.

Once you've created your spending plan, you need to document it with a simple spreadsheet or whatever financial tool you prefer. You might notice that I used the term "spending plan" as opposed to "budget." I prefer spending plan because I think it is a more powerful term and gives you a sense of being in control. Obviously, you can choose the term you like the best.

2. Understand Assets Versus Liabilities

Next up for the financially literate person is understanding the difference between an asset and a liability. I am going against what we have traditionally thought to be an asset. In the past, we have listed an asset as things we own such as a car, house, boat, etc. and then attached a value to that item. The problem arises when the marketplace is not willing to pay what we think the item is worth.

I prefer to go with the definitions Robert Kiyoaski gave in Rich Dad & Poor Dad many years ago.

Assets put money into your pocket while liabilities take money out.

Some examples of assets are:

- Income producing real estate
- Stocks that produce dividends
- Bonds
- Books/Songs that produce royalties
- Businesses

This is just a short list of assets.

Almost everything that we buy is a liability...some we buy out of necessity and others we purchase for enjoyment. Think of food, housing, cars, clothes, cell phones, and the list goes on.

In my experience, both financially literate and financially intelligent people are almost fanatical about either acquiring or creating assets. They understand that by having enough assets under their control they can easily create income that in turn will pay for their liabilities.

3. How to Use Debt Intelligently

The word debt brings up different thoughts and emotions for different people. For some, debt is something to avoid at all costs, while others see debt as a tool to be used as leverage. When it comes to real estate investing there are numerous ways to intelligently utilize lines of credit, home equity, hard money loans, and credit cards to purchase real estate assets.

But just like everything else in life, you must develop your own philosophy when it comes to the use of debt.

Personally, I only look to take on debt if it is going to make me money.

One of my pet peeves when it comes to this subject is that most financial experts paint the picture of debt freedom being the ultimate financial goal. And while that is not a bad thought. The real goal should be wealth, with debt freedom being a stop along the journey. See 2 Kings 4:1-7 if you want a biblical example of this concept. Consider the below statement:

One can be debt free, and still not be financially free.

I have learned that cash flow, not debt freedom, is the key to financial freedom. Teaching people how to create cash flow is far more important than teaching people how to become debt free.

Jumping back into real estate for a quick second; I have often seen real estate purchased with debt be used to fund a number of financial goals including the retiring of personal loans, student loans, car loans, etc. I already mentioned my friend earlier in this section, but let me share two other examples with you.

One of my early real estate mentors often talked about paying off thousands of dollars of student loans using real estate. Another friend of mine often talks about borrowing money to flip a house and then using the proceeds of the sale to eliminate their personal debt.

As you can see, they were smart about the utilization of debt, and it allowed them to retire both student loan and personal debts faster. One of the reasons I am writing this book is to help you become a Real Estate Wealth Creator in order to pay off your debts sooner.

4. Leverage the Power of Life Insurance

Life insurance is probably the financial instrument people love to talk least about. Most of us do not want to think about our own mortality. I have often said that just because we don't talk about death, does not mean it is not going to happen. Anyway, there are basically two types of life insurance: Term Insurance and Permanent Life Insurance. Their basic difference is that one offers strictly pure protection while the other offers both protection and a savings component.

Term Insurance is the product with pure protection, meaning that at the death of the insured, a death benefit or certain predetermined amount of money is left for a beneficiary. Term is often cheaper which may allow for a person to purchase more coverage.

Permanent Life Insurance (such as whole life, universal life, and variable life) gives you both a death benefit as well as the ability to have savings inside of your policy known as cash value accumulation. This cash value can be leveraged in several ways:

- Policy Loans: Borrow against the cash value of the policy, often at favorable interest rates, without a credit check. These loans can be used for any purpose, such as funding a business, paying for education, or covering emergencies.

- Policy Surrenders: Withdraw part of the cash value (partial surrender) or the entire cash value (full surrender), although this may reduce the death benefit and may have tax implications.

Another huge benefit of life insurance is that in most cases money can be passed on tax free. This is huge as both income and estate taxes can greatly impact how much your beneficiaries ultimately inherit.

Whether you choose to use one product over the other, or utilize both, understanding and leveraging the power of life insurance can enhance your financial strategy, offering both security and growth opportunities. If you want to learn more about life insurance, check out my video on the subject by scanning the QR code.

Watch video!

5. Utilize Both Personal and Business Credit

The utilization of both personal and business credit is another key indicator of increased financial intelligence and financial literacy. Let's start with personal credit. Personal credit consists of a 3-digit score ranging from 300-850 and is driven by the 5 factors below.

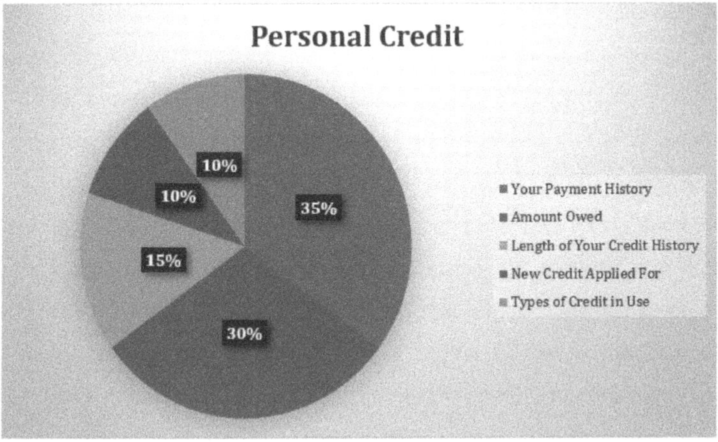

If you want to establish and or improve your credit, the 5 things above are what you must become proficient in.

Our personal credit scores, though only 3 little numbers, play an important part in many areas of our lives. Credit is often checked when it comes to renting apartments, screening potential employees, and calculating insurance premiums.

I have found that most people have a unique relationship with credit. On one hand, some are ignorant of the credit process and are hesitant to take steps to both improve or learn about their credit, while others have good, great, or even excellent credit and do absolutely nothing with that credit. This means they never use their credit to accelerate their wealth building or purchase assets such as real estate. I heard a speaker say this recently, "You can never brag about having a good credit score if you are not using it." I thought he was spot on with his assessment.

If you are looking for a rule of thumb around good to excellent credit. See below:

Good credit is 670-739

Very good is 740-799

Excellent is 800 and up

Business credit is actually what it sounds like. Your business establishes its own credit based on its dealings in the marketplace. When your business opens lines of credit, credit cards, and the like, it is establishing its own credit legacy. Business credit scores range from 1-100. Around 80 and above is considered to be a good business credit score.

Financially literate people understand the importance of separating their personal self from their business self. One of the ways you do this is by establishing business credit.

I only gave an overview of this subject. I suggest you do a deep dive on both personal and business credit as it will be of great benefit to you.

6. Maximize Their Earning Potential

Cranking up income generation in order to maximize earning potential is another thing the financially literate and financially intelligent do. In my opinion, most personal finance advice keeps people playing defense, meaning the advice focuses on things such as saving on your insurance coverage, budgeting, and living below your means. While all of these are important subjects, in my opinion they are all defensive strategies.

When you begin to talk about maximizing earning potential you are going on the offensive. And nowadays you have to go on the offensive in order to win the money game. I always teach people that they need to look to explode their income!

When you consider the statistics below, hopefully you can see why you must go on the offensive by maximizing your earning potential and exploding your income.

Wage Stagnation: Despite rising inflation, median household income in the U.S. only grew by 0.7% annually from 2010 to 2020.

Source: U.S. Census Bureau

Real Wage Decline: Adjusted for inflation, real wages have actually decreased by 3% from 2017 to 2022, meaning purchasing power has declined. *Source: Pew Research Center*

Cost of Living: The cost of living in major U.S. cities has increased by an average of 4% annually over the past decade, outpacing wage growth. *Source: Council for Community and Economic Research*

Hopefully, you are picking up what I am putting down. After waking people up to the current economic realities, the question always turns to, "How do I accomplish the goal of exploding my income?" First, you have to set an intention to do so. Nothing in life happens until we make up our minds that we are going to do something.

Secondly, whether you are an employee, entrepreneur, or both, you must find ways to deliver more value at a higher level. As an employee you must become a star player by finding ways to help your company increase their bottom line. This is done by showing your employer how you can help them save money or help them make more money. When you do this, you are distinguishing yourself from the mediocre masses.

Now that you have proven to be a star, it is time to begin negotiating for a promotion and/or raise or both. Being able to negotiate and sell yourself is a key skill to develop if you want to maximize your earning potential.

As a business owner, you have to deliver value to your clients and customers. You do this by solving their unique problems and filling their unique needs. When you do this, your customers and clients will pay you which is a receipt for a job well done. Also, as a business owner, you also have to serve the people working for you. Never forget that to truly run a business, you need committed others to help your enterprise succeed.

A word of caution in closing: no matter what category you find yourself in, when you explode your income, watch out for lifestyle creep. Just because you are making more money does not mean you have to spend more money. You want to use the excess for getting out of debt, cleaning up your credit, and more importantly for our next subject: investing.

7. Employ Their Money Through Investing

The financially literate and intelligent know that true wealth is a by-product of deploying and employing their dollars. The old saying is that there are only two forms of work:

1. You working for your money

2. Your money working for you

Whether you go the traditional investing route with 401Ks IRAs, stocks, bonds, etc. or choose to go a more unorthodox route, you must get your money working for you by becoming an investor. Investing, if done correctly, will allow you to make money while you sleep, give you time freedom, and allow you to defeat this thing we call inflation.

Since my goal is for you to become a Real Estate Wealth Creator, let me give you 3 ways to invest in real estate:

1. Become a buy and hold investor (We will be covering this a little later.)

2. Invest into large apartment complexes through syndications.

3. Lend your money to others for their real estate projects (You become like a bank.)

The above are 3 simple ways that I see people jumping into the real estate investing waters. There are other ways to get involved in real estate such as wholesaling or flipping. Those, in my opinion, are short term real estate monetization strategies and not investing.

You are probably wondering which is the best way for you to get started as a real estate investor. The answer depends on your goals and skillset and the time and money you have available as well as many other factors. If you want to explore what path may be best for your situation, start by taking our Real Estate Investor Readiness Assessment. Scan the QR code to begin:

8. Reduce and Eliminate Taxes

Last, but certainly not least, is financial literate and financially intelligent people learn how to keep more of their dollars through tax reduction and tax elimination. If there is any area of finances that ignorance is costly, it is definitely this one. Throughout the years I have said that debt, taxes, and inflation are your biggest financial enemies.

The bottom line is that you must get a decent handle on the tax code in order to defeat this enemy. You do this by hiring a tax strategist and not simply a tax preparer. A tax strategist is someone who you work with all year long to make strategic tax and money moves. A tax preparer you may only talk to once a year around tax time. If you are going to level up, you need a tax strategist.

Please understand that the tax code was designed to benefit business owners and real estate owners. One of the financial tips I heard a very rich man give many years ago was this:

Find out what the tax code rewards and operate accordingly.

You may be saying to yourself that the codes are not fair to employees. And you are probably right. But we can either sit around and cry about things not being fair or learn to successfully play the tax game. Anyway, I hope you are reading this book because your desire is to operate as an entrepreneur and real estate owner on some level. As I stated earlier, the tax code favors entrepreneurs and real estate owners. So, make sure to review the chapter on the 4 wealth generators as I shared some real estate wealth creation tax hacks. Also, let me recommend *Every Landlord's Tax Deduction Guide*. This outstanding resource can be purchased at Nolo.com.

Recap

Whew, that was a ton of information. Hopefully you can see how what we covered in this chapter relates to you becoming a Real Estate Wealth Creator. Many of the skills you will need to develop to succeed in real estate are in the list above. Speaking from my own experience in real estate, I can say this: creating spending plans, intelligently using debt, and developing a savvy tax strategy are essential to creating a successful real estate empire. Again, if you need help with some of the things we just talked about and desire to raise your level of financial intelligence and financial literacy, head over to DexterBJenkins.com.

Eight Areas of Financial Literacy: Notes

Go ahead and write down specific actions you need to take to improve in each of these areas.

1. Create a Spending Plan

2. Understand the Difference Between Asset and Liability

3. Use Debt Intelligently

4. Leverage Life Insurance

5. Manage Personal and Business Credit Properly

6. Maximize Your Earning Potential

7. Employ Money Through Investing

8. Reduce and Eliminate Taxes

Chapter Three Takeaways

- Financial intelligence and financial literacy combine the ability to understand a few basic financial concepts and then make wise decisions financially.
- There are 8 characteristics of financially literate and financially intelligent people.
- Cash flow, not debt freedom, is key to financial freedom.

4

The 4 Real Estate Wealth Generators

My real estate wealth creation journey started at around 9 years old with my parents buying their first home. I don't remember all the particulars but I do remember the home cost 30k dollars or as my dad said, a whole lot of haircuts. My dad was a barber and tended to measure the cost of things by the number of haircuts he had to perform to pay for an item. However, many thousands of haircuts it cost my dad, he found a nice home approximately fifteen minutes from Yale University in New Haven, Connecticut.

Like most Americans, now and then, it was always my parent's dream to own a house, but they wanted to be smart about it. That's why he chose to purchase a simple, two-family home instead of opting for a single-family home like over 4.3 million Americans do every year.

For the next decade, I watched my parents become both homeowners *and* landlords. My dad introduced me to the concept of house hacking before the term was even used. If you have never heard of the term, it simply describes someone who purchases a multi-unit property and lives in one of the units while renting out the others. In our case, we lived on the first floor while our tenants lived on the second floor. The power of house hacking is twofold.

1. **When applying for a mortgage, you can qualify for a bigger**

mortgage because the bank is counting a portion of the tenant's income along with yours.

2. **If you buy correctly, your tenant's rents should pay for all or most of the mortgage.**

This strategy — as simple as it is — was responsible for jump-starting my parent's wealth, my own wealth, and the wealth of many others I have met and taught throughout my life. If you don't learn anything else from this book, the idea of house hacking would be enough to turn you into a serious Real Estate Wealth Creator. House hacking is a major leverage play that can greatly assist you in your journey to financial success. The main problem for most is that house hacking means being a landlord which can be very tiring and a major headache. I won't lie to you — being a landlord is not easy, but it is more than worth the struggle. And you don't have to do it forever! Also, many people I know use property managers, who for a monthly fee, deal with the problems you do not want to.

House hacking strategically for one to two years gives you a major advantage. First, you should be cash-flowing enough to either provide additional needed income to use for savings and other financial goals you might want to accomplish. Secondly, in addition to cash flow, you are building something precious that we call equity. When you factor in living for free, the equity, and tax benefits you receive, being a landlord is not that bad. Remember, anything worth doing comes with a degree of aggravation. You get to choose your hard. Hard and broke, or hard and on the path to wealth.

My First Home

Fast forward the clock to 1999. I was no longer nine, but I found myself looking for my first property to purchase with my wife. My wife often mentions how I insisted on us buying a multi-family home. I do not remember ever saying those words, but the saying goes, *More is caught than taught!*

I do remember that living in a two-family home was the norm for me. I lived in one. The neighborhood I grew up in was full of them. However, my wife did not. She grew up in a home and many of her family members were homeowners, but they weren't landlords. It was something that she had to get used to, and looking back, I'm glad she did.

Our first multi-family home was a three-family home located in the Dorchester section of Boston. We purchased that home for just under 200k (a good deal even back then). We would live in that home for the next three years or so before mistakenly selling it for a nice profit. I say mistakenly because although we made a profit, I wasn't aware of how much money I had left on the table — I looked that home up recently and it's worth well over one million dollars. I left thousands of dollars of cashflow and more than $500,000 of appreciation on the table.

Remember this: *there is great power in buying great properties and allowing those properties to appreciate in value.*

Don't misunderstand me, I will never tell you that you shouldn't ever sell a property. There might be situations when selling just makes good business and life sense. A friend of my wife and I just sold a house they were living in because property values had skyrocketed, and they were planning on moving anyway because they wanted to downsize. They seized the opportunity the real estate market was affording them, took the money, and ran. This smart couple made a strategic wealth-building move by selling their house and it turned out pretty well for them.

The Four Real Estate Wealth Generators

There is tremendous wealth building power in real estate. One of my favorite sayings is that real estate is the lowest hanging fruit on the wealth building tree. Outside of inheriting wealth, real estate is, in my opinion, the simplest way to become wealthy. If one can develop the ability to grasp a few simple concepts and deploy a decent level of strategy and patience, real estate wealth is very attainable.

Let's begin to look at one of the concepts I learned early in my investing career and still lean quite heavily on today. If you are to become a Real Estate Wealth Creator, which is my stated goal for you, you must become familiar with the Four Real Estate Wealth Generators. I will refer to these four quite often in this book and for good reason. Everything my wife and I have built is based on these four principles. When you understand them and internalize them, it will be the basis of every single decision you make in your real estate career.

The first thing you must understand about the 4 Wealth Generators is that they work in tandem with what is known as a buy and hold strategy. Buying and holding is when you buy a piece of real estate, and that property becomes part of your real estate portfolio.

Wealth Generator #1: Cash Flow

Cash flow is the amount of cash left over after you have paid all the expenses associated with the property. Expenses may include mortgage payments, property taxes, insurance, property management fees, capital expenditures, etc.

The first question I ask myself when looking at a potential property to purchase is, "Will this property have positive monthly cash flow?" I don't believe that you should buy anything that does not have positive monthly cash flow, particularly when you are just starting out. Remember our goal is to become Real Estate Wealth Creators and cash flow is a huge part of that plan.

I am often asked what an acceptable amount of monthly cash flow is when purchasing real estate. There is no one set rule for this question as there are more than a few variables to consider. A few include where the property is located, what region of the country or state you are operating your business in, and the experience level of the investor — and that is just a partial list. So, it really just depends.

Most investors aim for a set amount per door or per unit. You will hear figures upwards of $100 per door/per unit to whatever an investor can earn.

For example, just say you buy a 3-unit property in a decent neighborhood and after all expenses have been paid you have $450 a month in positive cash flow. This means you are earning a $150 per door/per unit.

This $450 monthly positive cash flow equals an additional $5,400 a year.

Is that a decent profit? Again, it depends on what you want to earn as a profit.

Something to consider though is that you did no extra work to earn the additional $450 per month or $5,400 per year. How long would you have to work at your job in order to earn an extra $450 dollars per month or $5,400 per year? For most people they could not even quantify how to do what I just mentioned. Please grab ahold of what I am about to say as it is of extreme importance.

If you want to become wealthy, you must stop trading hours for dollars.

Your income generation must be disconnected from your direct involvement if wealth is your desire. This way of thinking is a huge departure from how most of us were trained as we were growing up. When you learn how to do this, you are well on your way to financial and, more importantly, time freedom. Real estate cash flow provides another source of income that you do not physically have to work for.

Wealth Generator #2: Appreciation

Appreciation, which comes in two forms, is a major player in your wealth creation toolbox. There is forced appreciation, which is when you make improvements to the dwelling, and it becomes more valuable. Forced appreciation is an active strategy that involves making specific improvements to a property to enhance its value. This could include adding additional living space, renovating outdated areas like kitchens and bathrooms, or enhancing the property's curb appeal. These targeted investments can significantly increase a property's worth and rental income potential. The other type of appreciation is natural appreciation. This happens gradually as market conditions cause the property to appreciate over time. This can be due to factors like economic development in the area, increased demand for housing, or inflation. Natural appreciation is less predictable but can significantly contribute to long-term wealth creation as the property value increases without additional investment from the owner.

Throughout the years I have both seen and experienced the benefits of both types of appreciation. The properties in New Haven that my father purchased for about 110K are worth well over 600K today, which is a conservative estimate.

And in 2018, a property that my wife and I bought for 217K and put 60k in improvements is worth over 500K. As I said earlier, appreciation, if understood and applied, is a major player in helping you to grow your wealth. I would strongly encourage you to at least consider taking on property or two that need some renovation. By successfully taking on properties that need some love, you can really accelerate your wealth building.

Even if you prefer not to get involved in rehabbing and choose to buy properties that are pretty much turnkey, you still can become a Real Estate Wealth Creator. Over the last 30 years, real estate has appreciated at about a 3 percent rate which not only grows your wealth but serves as an excellent inflation hedge.

Wealth Generator #3 Tax Benefits

In order to build wealth, you must always be looking for ways to legally, and strategically, reduce your taxes. Debt, taxes, and inflation are in my opinion the big 3 when it comes to personal wealth reduction. Owning real estate and becoming a Real Estate Wealth Creator will allow you to take advantage of things such as deductible expenses, depreciation, and 1031 exchanges. America's tax laws change over time, but the tax code has always favored land and business owners.

Understanding Deductible Expenses

One of the best parts of real estate is the deduction of expenses. These deductible expenses include but are not limited to:

- Mortgage interest
- Property taxes
- Operating expenses (utilities, property management fees, maintenance, repairs)
- Insurance premiums
- Advertising expenses for finding tenants

Understanding which expenses are deductible and meticulously tracking them throughout the year can significantly reduce your taxable income from real estate investments.

Wealth Generator #4: Debt Paydown

The best way to think of debt paydown in real estate investment is as an enforced savings plan, where the principal portion of the mortgage payment is paid down over time through the income generated from tenants. This process gradually increases the investor's equity in the property without requiring additional out-of-pocket contributions.

As tenants continue to pay rent, they indirectly contribute to reducing the mortgage balance, allowing the investor to build wealth through increased property ownership. This benefit is most pronounced when using leverage to purchase the property, as it combines the use of borrowed funds to accelerate wealth accumulation while the asset itself appreciates in value. While purchasing a property outright can lead to stronger immediate cash flow due to the absence of mortgage payments, utilizing debt strategically allows for the benefits of leverage, including the potential for higher returns on investment through appreciation and tax deductions, alongside the gradual build-up of equity through debt paydown.

Putting It All Together

By now, we have established that real estate is one of the best tools for increasing your wealth. But it's only as powerful as the person using it. First, you must believe with every fiber in your body that you are a Real Estate Wealth Creator. Second, by understanding and utilizing cash flow, appreciation, tax benefits, and debt paydown, you will without a doubt form a real estate strategy that will help you build tremendous wealth for you and your family.

Chapter Four Takeaways

- House hacking produces major financial leverage and can act as a catalyst for Real Estate Wealth Creation.

- To achieve financial freedom, stop trading time for money.
- Buy and hold investing works powerfully when paired with The Four Real Estate Wealth Generators.

5

How Do I Get Started as a Real Estate Wealth Creator?

"The only mistake you cannot overcome in real estate investing is the mistake of not getting started." Dexter B. Jenkins

The above quote is one of my top 3 real estate investing truths. I mentioned the first truth earlier in the book. So, to kick off this chapter I am putting all three truths together.

1. **Real estate is the lowest-hanging fruit on the wealth creation tree.**

2. **The only mistake you cannot overcome in real estate investing is the mistake of not getting started.**

3. **You need coaching or mentoring to succeed on your real estate investing journey.**

The next few chapters are going to center around both the intangible and tangible things needed to get you started as a Real Estate Wealth Creator. The principle of getting started is one that I take extremely seriously and think most people completely miss. I am such a big believer in the getting started principle that I deemed the year 2023 "The Year of Getting Started" in both my church and personal life.

Let me go deeper around this getting started thing. Even though you and I have not personally met yet, there are two things that I can confidently say about you.

1. **You are a lifelong learner (most people stop reading after high school or college.)**

2. **You are most likely a pretty accomplished person.**

I am not going to say much regarding point number 1, but it does tie perfectly into my truth on coaching or mentoring. Books are a very inexpensive way to receive coaching and mentoring. If you want to become a Real Estate Wealth Creator, you must become a reader on some level.

But delving deeper into this thought around you being a pretty accomplished person. However, you choose to define success and accomplishment, I can safely say you have reached certain milestones because you tapped into the principle of getting started.

Everything accomplishment I have listed below took place because you got started:

- High school graduation

- College graduation

- Earning an MBA

- Starting a successful business

- Starting a non-profit

- Having a family

- Anything else you are proud of

Of course, it can be argued that you had to have the determination to be a finisher which is true. But one cannot finish with determination what they failed to get started.

Let's talk about the 4 intangible pillars needed to get you started as a Real Estate Wealth Creator.

4 Pillars of Getting Started as a Real Estate Wealth Creator

1. Intention

The first pillar is intention or decision. Most people never decide that they are going to become Real Estate Wealth Creators. If I had a dollar for every time I have met someone who said, "I always wanted to get involved in real estate," I would be an extremely wealthy man. Being casual about this thing is not going to cut it.

I believe setting your intention, or deciding, begins with having a goal or establishing your Big Why. These are a must because they will keep you motivated and act as your life raft as you deal with the adversities of real estate investing.

Back in 2016, I remember clearly when I decided that I was going to become a Real Estate Wealth Creator. While up reading one night, I decided that I was going to seriously pursue real estate investing. My goal or Big Why centered around wanting to leave an inheritance for my children and not wanting to squander the real estate assets I would inherit from my dad. In my heart I knew at that moment I did not have the skill sets to accomplish either of those goals.

Setting my intention and keeping my focus on my Big Why has successfully carried us through the pandemic of 2020. This was an extremely challenging time for our business as well as for most real estate investors. We had to deal with people shortages, supply chain issues, along with the general fear that gripped our country. Despite all that I just mentioned we were able to keep our business moving and be quite productive during that time.

2. Education

The second pillar is the necessity of acquiring real estate investing education. One cannot learn this business on your own which is why I introduced my third real estate investing truth earlier.

You must make up your mind that you are going to become a student of this industry. I break educational options into two basic categories. The first is there are free or almost free educational resources such as the library, YouTube, podcasts, social media online groups, meetups, and REIA groups. REIA stands for real estate investment associations, and they often have a small membership fee for being a part of the association. You should be able to google and find your local REIA groups with no problem.

To illustrate the power of REIA groups: a friend of mine, who is also an investor and lender, shared how one of his recent clients had earned 70K on a fix and flip project. The young man was only 22 years old and doing his first project. The REIA he belonged to became a one stop shop for this young man. The project was brought to him by a person in his group, he found an investing partner in the group, and the hard money loan was sourced in the group. There is tremendous power in being part of the right communities.

The other category is paid coaching and or mentorships. The great thing about mentors and coaches is their ability to help accelerate your success. If you are like me, you want your success — and you want it yesterday.

My wife and I joined a paid coaching program, and it has paid off for us tremendously. Not only did we gain knowledge from our mentors, but their networks became our networks. That alone has saved us a ton of money on our projects and enabled us to connect with other like-minded investors. In my opinion paying for coaching or mentorship is like buying into a franchise.

My parting words on this subject are to 1) Properly vet any program you are considering. Check them out with the Better Business Bureau to see if the company has any legitimate complaints against it. 2) Make sure the instructors have a proven track record and care about your success. 3) Never be afraid to make an investment in yourself which is what you are doing through their program. 4) Make sure you do the work as nothing works unless you work it.

3. Courage

The third intangible pillar is this thing called courage. I promised in the subtitle that I would give you keys to overcome a number of things with fear being one of them. Fear is probably the biggest reason why most never become Real Estate Wealth Creators.

The antidote to fear is this force called courage. Let me give you my definition of courage.

COURAGE is the willingness to confront fears, doubts, and insecurities in order to accomplish a particular task.

I believe this is a great definition, because as you are starting on this journey to become a Real Estate Wealth Creator, you are going to have to confront fear, doubt, and insecurity.

The great thing about courage is that, like a muscle, it can be cultivated or grown. Every time you confront something you are afraid of your courage muscle grows. Confronting fear has the same effect on your courage that a bicep curl has on your biceps.

You may wonder how fear stops us as Real Estate Wealth Creators. This is how: Fear acts as a bully and causes one to ask disempowering questions such as:

What if I lose my money on a project?

Where am I going to find good tradespeople?

What if I get bad tenants?

What if the contractor runs off with my money?

How am I going to become a real estate investor at my age?

What if the economy tanks?

What if the market shifts?

What if I receive bad treatment from a seller or buyer?

This is only a partial list of disempowering questions. I am quite sure you can come up with your own list. Never forget that one cannot get a positive and empowered result asking disempowering questions. Everything on the list above is a distinct possibility and can be overcome and defeated by the things we are talking about in this chapter, including courage.

I am well aware that as you are starting out on your real estate investing journey, the temptation to be afraid is present. We are talking about you stepping into something completely and absolutely new and that there is the potential for the loss of tens of thousands of dollars. I remember closing on our first deal back in 2017 like it was yesterday. My wife and I were sitting in between two lawyers signing papers left and right. I began thinking to myself that this real estate investing thing is no longer theory but reality. In other words, it was time to put up or shut up. Well, I can tell you that since that day, we have grown our courage muscle, and have been involved in numerous real estate transactions since then.

If you want to know more about developing courage to succeed in business and in life. I have included a bonus piece on the subject.

4. Community

The last but not least intangible of getting started is the power of community. I always laugh to myself when I hear people being introduced as self-made anything. The truth is that from our birth, till our death, we are all interdependent beings and need each other. This is especially true when it comes to becoming a Real Estate Wealth Creator. If you are going to succeed in this business, you are going to need to tap into the power of community.

In my opinion, this is what constitutes a community:

A community is 2 or more people coming together in order to provide support, expertise, resources, and accountability, thereby enabling individuals to accomplish a task or goal.

Communities, among other things, have the ability to help you go further and faster, they have the ability to inspire you to become more and to do more, and they also have the ability to grow your confidence and courage.

Hopefully the first community you have or develop is in your home. My wife and children have been extremely supportive of all of my entrepreneurial endeavors. If that is not your situation for whatever reason, my suggestion is to seek out a supportive community by any ethical means necessary at your church, through your networking, and through the attending of events.

So far, we have covered the intangibles of getting started. In the next chapter we are going to talk about team building.

Chapter Five Takeaways

- The only mistake you cannot overcome in real estate investing is the mistake of not getting started.

- There are 4 pillars when it comes to the intangibles of getting started as a Real Estate Wealth Creator.

- You cannot receive an empowered result asking disempowering questions.

6

Building Your Real Estate Wealth Creation Team

Now on to the tangible side of getting started. As a Real Estate Wealth Creator, you will be utilizing what I call the FFM Formula. FFM stands for:

- **Finding Deals**
- **Funding Deals**
- **Monetizing Deals**

Just so we can all be on the same page, below is how I define a deal in real estate.

A deal is a located piece of real estate that I control or purchase that will allow me to achieve my real estate objectives.

The above definition will mean more to you as we go along, but the team that you assemble should help you to tap into the FFM formula.

I am often asked who should be on a real estate wealth creation team. I am going to give you your starting 5 and then list 6 others that should be on your roster.

Real Estate Agents

Agents can and should be a major source of finding deals for your business. Though they will not be your only source as deals can and will come from many places. With that being said, working with the rights agents can be a major plus for your business. While any agent might be able to bring you a deal, you really want to look for investor-friendly agents. These agents have experience working with investors and sometimes they are investors themselves. When networking with agents, I ask if they have experience working with investors or are investors themselves. Two other things to note:

1. **You will find many investor-friendly agents at REIA's and real estate related meetups.**
2. **You might want to consider becoming an agent yourself.**

Signing up with an office that has other investor/agents can accelerate your growth as a Real Estate Wealth Creator.

Deals and Agents

Jumpstarting your deal finding can be as simple as reaching out to the top agents in your area of investing interest. Finding these agents is as simple as looking on Zillow or paying attention to the realtor yard signs in your identified area. If a person's name continually shows up, they are a serious player. When you touch base with them, establish that you are an investor looking for properties that are in a distressed condition. These distressed properties are often in disrepair, have high grass, old cars in the driveway, etc. These are the properties that the average or retail buyer does not want anything to do with. Also, these properties are often a pain for agents as they are much harder to sell. Sometimes agents keep these as pocket listings. Pocket listings are houses that have not been listed publicly due to the condition of the property or for some other reason. In these situations, you can come in and become a welcome solution for both sellers and agents.

As Real Estate Wealth Creators, the ugly, cat pee smelling, dated, and in some cases totally dilapidated properties are the ones we go after. And the right agents can help you find these.

Remember this:

We get paid to run toward what others run from.

Lawyers

Lawyers, like agents, are integral to your business as they handle the legal aspects of a real estate transaction. Depending on your state of operation you may be dealing with a title company as opposed to an attorney. Anyway, a lawyer's main job is to help you get to the closing table, which is why having a lawyer who is used to working with real estate investors is helpful. Many things can happen during a real estate transaction and often flexibility and creativity are key to keeping deals from falling apart.

Also, lawyers can also be a great source of deals for your business. Sometimes a portion of a person's practice will include estate planning. You can become an extension of their business by helping them to move unwanted real estate their clients may have inherited. Think of a scenario where someone inherits a piece of property from a relative but lives out of state or just does not have the time or ability to deal with the real estate. You can step in and become a problem solver for someone in this situation. Having gone through the estate settling process twice, I can tell you from firsthand experience that this can be an overwhelming time. You are navigating a number of things including your emotions, difficult relatives, as well as financial and legal issues.

General Contractors and Tradespeople

Projects can vary from being a total rehab to some simple updating to new construction. Either way you will need individuals to work on your projects. Let me tell you — good tradespeople are worth their weight in gold. Some of the people you will need, depending on the project, will be plumbers, electricians, carpenters, masons, painters, etc. Architects and structural engineers might also be called for as drawings and structural issues might come into play.

Don't get overwhelmed at the thought of having to find all these individuals. If you hire a general contractor, he or she will have teams of people that will include all of the above. GCs, as they are called, have a special designation and can oversee your project for a fee which frees you up to continue to run your business and do other things.

On all of our projects we have had the benefit of working with great, investor-friendly GCs. These individuals understand that you are in the business of creating a great product without breaking the bank. Often, they will also be able to make suggestions that will enhance your overall project.

I believe in the Noah's Ark theory when it comes to this business. You need two or more of everything. Always be on the look-out for quality tradespeople. Life happens and you don't want to be caught without someone else you can call to get work done.

To illustrate the realness of the life happens concept, our first GC, who did 4 projects for us, moved with his family to North Carolina which was a tremendous loss for us. And on another project we were consulting on, the GC had a heart attack and died. Again, life happens so always be looking and recruiting.

The best way I have found tradespeople is through referrals. Ask people in your sphere of influence who they use and ask for an introduction.

Make sure to properly vet them by checking their license and insurance information. Many states have sites you can check to verify license status and to see if any legal complaints have been filed against them or their company. Also, do not forget to inquire about past projects they have completed. Contacting former clients and tastefully driving by to check out finished projects is advisable.

Funding Partners

All your real estate transactions will need to be funded or paid for. There are times when it makes sense to use your own cash, lines of credit, or home equity. Let me speak quickly about the power of properly using home equity as many are reluctant to use this precious commodity. By tapping into the equity of your home using a HELOC or cash out refinance. It could be the cash you need to get your business off the ground. In reality though, most of your business will be run by using other people's money (OPM). Funding sources can and will range from sources like banks and credit unions to hard money lenders and private individuals.

Different money sources will require different things in order to fund your deal. Banks and credit unions tend to look more at the investor and their creditworthiness while hard money lenders and private money sources look more at the deal.

Banks and credit unions tend to be a lot slower in their underwriting while the other sources can move a lot faster. Each has its pros and cons so you will have to assess which way to go based on the deal.

Again, have a number of these funding partners at your disposal. Also, do not let money stop you from getting started. The main thing you will need in your real estate business is creativity and resourcefulness. There are always ways to fund projects if your desire is strong enough. Please remember this:

Creativity and resourcefulness will always overcome the lack of money and resources.

Let me give you an example of mixing strong desire together with creativity and resourcefulness. The leader of the main REIA I attend often talks about being a recent divorcée and wanting to purchase a home. Not having much money, she did some marketing and came across a distressed homeowner who was willing to sell her their house on a subject to deal. A subject to deal is when the owner allows you to take over the current mortgage while signing the deed over to you. This allows you to have ownership of the property without having to qualify for a mortgage. This type of transaction some would consider to be a more advanced purchase strategy. So, I do not have time to totally break down how these types of deals work. The bottom line was that my friend, through creativity and resourcefulness, created a win-win solution for both her and the homeowner as the previous owner was dealing with a sick spouse and needed relief. That is the power of creativity and resourcefulness in action.

Back to the subject of hard money borrowing for a minute; this is one of the hardest concepts to grasp for newer investors as this type of lending is very different. For that reason, I put together a free resource on hard money lending. Access that resource by visiting *DexterBJenkins.com/HardMoneyLending*.

Tax Professionals

To round out your starting five, you're going to need a competent tax professional who knows how to work with real estate investors. As we said earlier, real estate offers a ton of tax benefits, and you'll want to take advantage of them all.

Thus far we have covered your starting. Below are the other 6 players I mentioned earlier and how they fit into your Real Estate Wealth Creator game plan.

1. **Property Manager:** Manages the day-to-day operations of rental properties.
2. **Insurance Agent:** Ensures properties are properly insured.
3. **Mentor or Coach:** Provides experienced guidance and advice.
4. **Bookkeeper/Accountant:** Manages financial records and provides financial insights.
5. **Appraiser:** Assesses the value of properties to ensure fair pricing.
6. **Home Inspector:** Identifies potential issues in properties before purchase.

Monetization

Finally, we are down to the monetization part of our formula. The great part about real estate is that there are so many ways to make money in this business. This can also become a hindrance as you can become the victim of the shiny object syndrome and never get any real traction.

As a Real Estate Wealth Creator, you must have multiple exit and monetization strategies. Depending on what happens in the real estate market, you might have to pivot and do something other than what you initially planned. I am going to talk about the three common ways most people earn income as Real Estate Wealth Creators and then introduce some others that you might want to explore.

Buy and Hold Investing

We spoke briefly on buy and hold earlier, so we are going to touch on this again quickly. Buy and hold is when you purchase a property with the intent of keeping it for the positive cashflow. Cash flow is king and a major key to you building long term wealth. If done correctly, buying, and holding can and should become what is called passive income. Though nothing is ever quite passive, because of the need for things to be managed, it sure is sweet to wake up around the first of every month and see that rent deposits have been made to your bank account. Earning money in this fashion breaks you out of the trading hours for dollars method of making money.

Buy and hold investing can take the form of traditional investing where you purchase a piece of real estate and rent it out to a tenant. Or you can tap into non-traditional ways to become a buy and hold investor. I have listed some of those options in our next section. This is my big thought on the subject:

Buy and hold investing is where long term wealth is built.

Going back to my father for a moment, I recall a conversation he and I had where I mentioned that one of his long-term tenants had paid him $800 dollars for 20 years. Dad made the mistake many make in not raising rents periodically to keep up with inflation. You also want to do this if you want to refinance or sell. But these are lessons for another day.

After doing the math, which was $800 dollars x 20 years, we discovered that this one tenant had paid him about $192,000 over that period of time. Also, this property had an additional rental unit, 4 garages, and was the property dad ran his barbershop out of.

If you go back to the chapter on the 4 wealth generators and grasp the power of my dad's example, you can see that buy and hold investing is a serious wealth builder.

Fixing and Flipping

This is when you purchase a property with the intent of doing some renovations and selling it to a retail buyer. Depending on your personality, business model, and other factors, the renovations could be major or minor in scope. The key to this strategy is to buy the property at a price that, after all the renovations and money expenses are paid out, you will be able to make a profit from. Profits are earned on the purchase but not realized until the sale of the property. This is where many investors make their mistake. They do not factor in as many of the expenses as they should and end up losing money on their deals. It is impossible to factor in everything as surprises come up but do the best you can. Following some sort of checklist is helpful when you are doing a fix and flip. I suggest checking within your local REIA or talking with other investors to see if they have a checklist you might be able to use.

Fixing and flipping is a speed game as you want to get in and out of projects within 6 -12 months depending on the scope of the project. From the moment that you close on the property, there must be a sprint to get the project renovated and sold, often because you have taken out short term financing through a hard money lender or private investor. This helps to keep your feet to the fire so to speak.

Fixing and flipping is also where you make your big checks. The biggest checks that we have seen in this business have been as a result of fixing and flipping.

Wholesaling

This is when you find a distressed property or distressed owner and, often without owning the house, assign the contract to buy the property to an end buyer. Most real estate contracts are assignable unless the contract explicitly forbids it. This means another party can step in and take your place in the transaction. You are essentially playing matchmaker by bringing a seller and buyer together. And, because of your efforts, you earn a predetermined sum. Wholesaling is not considered investing by most but is a viable exit or income strategy.

Many people get their start in real estate investing through wholesaling as you often don't need a ton of money to get started. Wholesalers number 1 skill is the ability to find deals which in my opinion is the number 1 skill you will have to master to have long term success.

The common denominator between the 3 monetization strategies I just covered is this thing called marketing. In order to have success on any level in this business, you must become proficient in marketing or get connected with someone who is. Becoming a Real Estate Wealth Creator is going to require you to become a serious marketer.

I shared with you the big three monetization strategies. Below I have listed below a number of other strategies to consider.

Other Monetization Strategies

Real Estate Crowdfunding: Invest in real estate projects through crowdfunding platforms where multiple investors pool their money to fund large projects. Returns can come from rental income or property appreciation.

REITs (Real Estate Investment Trusts): Invest in publicly traded REITs which own, operate, or finance income-generating real estate. This provides a way to earn dividends without directly owning property.

Lease Options: Purchase a property with an option to lease it to a tenant who has the option to buy it at a predetermined price within a specific timeframe. You earn from the lease payments and a potential sale premium.

Tax Lien Investing: Buy tax lien certificates from local governments. If the property owner fails to pay their taxes, you can earn interest on your investment and potentially acquire the property.

Vacation Rentals: Invest in properties to be used as short-term vacation rentals through platforms like Airbnb or VRBO. These properties often yield higher returns due to short-term rental premiums.

Real Estate Syndication: Partner with other investors in a syndicate to collectively purchase larger properties. As an indicator, you can earn acquisition fees, management fees, and a share of the profits.

Commercial Real Estate: Invest in commercial properties like office buildings, retail spaces, or warehouses. These properties can provide stable rental income and longer lease terms compared to residential properties.

Real Estate Notes: Purchase real estate notes, which are loans secured by property. You earn income from the interest payments made by the borrower, and potentially from acquiring the property if the borrower defaults.

Self-Storage Units: Invest in self-storage facilities which can provide a steady cash flow from rental fees. These investments often have lower maintenance costs and higher returns.

Mobile Home Parks: Purchase and manage mobile home parks. This niche market can provide significant cash flow with lower per-unit costs and higher tenant stability.

Private Money Lending: Act as a private money broker by lending your own funds or raising funds from other investors to provide short-term loans to other real estate investors. You earn interest on the loan and can charge origination fees.

Real Estate Development: Engage in developing raw land or redeveloping existing properties. This can include residential subdivisions, commercial projects, or mixed-use developments. Profits are generated from the sale or lease of the developed properties.

Property Management: Start a property management business to manage rental properties for other investors. You earn income through management fees and sometimes by taking a percentage of the rental income.

Real Estate Consulting: Offer your expertise as a consultant to other investors or property owners. This can include advising on property acquisitions, market analysis, investment strategies, or project management.

Real Estate Auctions: Participate in real estate auctions to buy properties below market value. You can then resell these properties at a higher price or improve them to increase their value before selling.

Real Estate Partnerships: Form partnerships with other investors where each partner contributes different resources (capital, expertise, labor) to acquire and manage properties. Profits are shared among the partners.

Rent-to-Own Programs: Set up rent-to-own programs where tenants rent a property with the option to purchase it after a set period. You earn rental income and a potential sale premium.

Agricultural Land Investment: Invest in agricultural land that can be leased to farmers. This can provide steady rental income and potential appreciation in land value.

Real Estate Marketing and Sales: Specialize in marketing and selling real estate properties for developers, banks, or other investors. You earn commissions from sales transactions.

Real Estate Technology Solutions: Invest in or develop technology solutions that serve the real estate industry, such as property management software, real estate investment platforms, or virtual tour technology. Revenue can come from software sales, subscriptions, or service fees.

Conclusion

We've covered a lot in this chapter, and by now, you should have a clear understanding of who should be on your real estate team and how to build it effectively. Remember, the strength of your team will directly impact your ability to find, fund, and monetize deals efficiently. Surround yourself with experts, and you'll be well on your way to becoming a successful Real Estate Wealth Creator.

In Chapter 7, we will explore how to synthesize everything you've learned into a cohesive strategy that will guide your real estate investments moving forward. Get ready to put all the pieces together and take decisive action to achieve your financial goals.

Chapter Six Takeaways

- As a Real Estate Wealth Creator, you will be using the FFM Formula.
- Your Wealth Creator team should leverage the FFM Formula.
- There are 5 primary players on your team and 6 more who should be on your roster.
- There are three main monetization strategies you will use as a Real Estate Wealth Creator.

7

Time for Action

Congratulations! You have made it to the final chapter. You are now ready to go and take action. Action is where the rubber meets the road. I am a firm believer in the following statement.

Information without implementation brings frustration.

In this chapter I want to help you begin to implement a few things that will help you become a Real Estate Wealth Creator. The bottom line is this: everything we have talked about is simply theory until you move into implementation mode.

So, with that in mind, I am going to pretend that you and I are sharing a meal and you have asked, "What do I need to do to get started?" Here is my answer.

1. Decide you are going to become a real estate investor. You must make the decision that you are going to do this business. When you decide, you are telling yourself and others that, come hell or high water, you are going to make it happen. I am going to refer back to what I stated in the introduction: as a Real Estate Wealth Creator, you have decided that you are going to use real estate as a primary wealth creation tool. As part of your decision making, I would also encourage you to take our free Real Estate Investor Readiness Assessment. You can access here at *DexterBJenkins.co*

m/REIassessment.

2. Decide what you want this business to produce for you. In other words, what is your Why? There must be something that you strongly desire to achieve in order to win. Whatever your goals are, real estate investing can be the avenue for its achievement. Are your aspirations to:

- Leave a legacy of wealth and success
- Work on your own schedule and enjoy time freedom
- Be your own boss
- Spend more time with my family
- Reach your fullest financial potential
- Be the go-to financial person in your family
- Retire your spouse
- Retire your parents
- Pay for college education
- Build a second stream of income
- Travel the world whenever you want
- Buy a vacation home

I have no clue as to what your Why is, but it is imperative that you have one. Another way to come up with your Why is to answer this question: *Who will you not quit on?*

All of us have the tendency to give up on ourselves at times. But if we focus on that person or persons that we hold in our hearts. We will develop the needed tenacity to keep moving. However, you come with your Why. Write it down and look at it constantly.

3. Invest the time, energy, and money educating yourself to become a Real Estate Wealth Creator. To improve any area of life you must be willing to invest the assets I just mentioned. Books, Reia groups, meetups, networking events, podcasts, masterminds, and mentors are all avenues for your education. As you begin to educate yourself, your teachers will become plain to you. I said it earlier, but in bears repeating: I believe investing in mentorship as this accelerates your success. Even if funds are low, discover how you can be an asset to someone who is more successful than you in this field. In exchange for whatever value you can bring that person, ask if they can teach you how to become a Real Estate Wealth Creator.

4. Get out there and mix it up in these real estate investing streets. Go start looking at properties, networking with realtors, wholesalers, and other investors. This is a business of doing to learn. These concepts only come to life when you get in real live conversations with sellers, begin to put in offers with realtors, talk with funders and contractors, etc. When I first started, I had a goal of walking through two properties a week. After walking the properties, I would go over the numbers to see if it would be a good property to purchase to fix and flip. I would also call up other real estate investors to see if I could walk their current project. You really just want to get in motion.

5. Take down your first real estate transaction, whether it be a wholesale deal, a fix and flip, or a buy and hold property. The goal of the first deal is not to make a ton of money but to have proof of concept. Of course, you want to make money as we are in business. But I have seen people give up

after one deal did not go as they expected. If you are going to succeed you need to develop some grit and resilience.

6. Enjoy the fact that you completed your first transaction and share it with the world. One of the things you want to begin to do is document your real estate investing journey. If you are a social media person, I suggest that you let folks know that you are a real estate investor. I have been able to attract tons of opportunities because I let people know that I am into real estate through my social media accounts. If you want to follow me, I am Dexter B. Jenkins across all the social media platforms. I may have not talked about this enough in this book, but you will quickly find out that you are not only in real estate, but you are also in marketing. Make yourself findable!

7. Rinse and repeat steps 1 through 6.

I have said all I am going to say for now. If you take the information and follow the steps I gave you in this book, you can become a Real Estate Wealth Creator. Of course this is not all the knowledge you will need, but it will get you headed in the right direction. Understand that you are in the process of reinventing yourself which does not happen overnight. But I am fully persuaded that if you stick with it, you will enjoy good success and enjoy the spoils of becoming a Real Estate Wealth Creator.

I look forward to hearing your real estate success story very soon.

Chapter Seven Takeaways

- Information without implementation brings frustration.
- Again, decide what you want and take action.
- Follow seven practical steps to getting started as a Real Estate Wealth Creator.

Real Estate Glossary of Terms

Every vocation has words or vocabulary one must master in order to succeed. Real estate is no different. We have included a list of words that you will find helpful as you are conducting business. It is suggested to keep this list nearby so you can easily research terms that are foreign to you.

A

Absentee Landlord — This term refers to a landlord that owns and rents out a property to earn profit and does not live on the property or in the local economic region.

Abstract of Title — This is the summary that provides details of the title deeds and documents that prove the seller/owner's right to dispose of the property.

Adjustable-Rate Mortgage (ARM) — An adjustable-rate mortgage is a type of mortgage in which the rate of the outstanding balance varies throughout the life of the loan. With an adjustable-rate mortgage, it is more difficult for the borrower to predict and plan for monthly payments. Traditionally, the initial interest rate will be fixed for a certain period of time until it resets based on the current interest rates.

Adverse Possession — Is a legal doctrine that allows a person to claim a property right in land owned by another. Common examples of adverse possession include continuous use of a private road or driveway, or agricultural development of an unused parcel of land. By favoring the adverse possessor over the true landowner, the doctrine of adverse possession rewards the productive use of land and punishes landowners who "sleep on their rights."

After Repair Value (ARV) — This estimates the future value of the property after renovations and any repairs that are made to the property. This is not the value of the property at purchase but following the improvements that are made to the property and is an estimation, not a guarantee, based on what comparable properties have recently sold for.

Amenity — An amenity is a desirable or useful feature or facility within a property structure. Amenities are typically features that are highlighted and pitched to renters when they are looking to rent at a certain complex. Amenities can also be found within gated communities or other areas that have an HOA when talking about single family homes, townhomes, or condos. Examples include a pool, workout room, on-site laundry facilities, etc.

Amortization — This is the process of spreading out a loan into a series of fixed payments over a period of time. Although a purchaser's total payment remains equal each period, the loan's interest and principal will be paid off in different amounts each month.

Appraisal — An appraisal will typically happen during escrow or if a person is refinancing their home. It is an unbiased professional opinion of a home's value, based on recently sold properties nearby.

Appraised Value — Is the estimated amount from an unbiased professional of the property's value.

Appraiser — An unbiased professional who is contracted during the escrow or refinance process to assess the value of the property in question.

Appreciation — Is the increase in a home's value over time. A home's appreciation can be calculated based on the fair market value of comparable homes in the neighborhood of the property in question. Appreciation of a home can come through the natural appreciation of the value of the home over time or can be forced into the home through upgrades, remodels, or renovations that add value to the home.

APR — Stands for annual percentage rate that is charged to the borrower. It is expressed as a percentage that represents the actual yearly cost of funds over the term of the loan.

Assessed Value — The assessed value is different from the appraised value in that it is the dollar value assigned to the property to measure applicable taxes. This determines the value of a property for tax purposes and takes comparable property sales and inspections of the property into consideration.

Asset Protection — Is a part of one's financial planning in order to protect one's assets from creditor claims. Both individuals and businesses use this technique to make sure they limit creditors access to claim valuable assets.

B

Bad Title — A bad title is when the current sellers are not granted the ownership of title due to a multitude of reasons. These can be either legal or financial problems that lead to a bad title and therefore can prevent the seller from being able to sell the asset.

Balloon Mortgage — A balloon mortgage is a fixed rate, typically low payment loan, with a large remainder due at the end of the loan period. Frequently, these loans are re-amortized before the balloon payment comes due.

Bank Owned Property — A bank owned property is one that is taken back into a bank's inventory after the owner defaults on the mortgage loan. This type of property is likely to be sold at a discounted price or lower than other comparable properties in the same location.

Broker — A real estate broker is not the same thing as a real estate agent. A broker is an agent who has also passed their broker license exam. The main difference between the two is that a real estate broker can also own a real estate agency or firm. Real estate agents are the ones that work for a real estate broker firm.

Broker Price Opinion — A broker price opinion is a report by a real estate agent or broker that is used to support the professional and unbiased opinion that helps determine the potential selling price. Based on comparable properties nearby that have sold recently, a BPO is used frequently by banks to price their properties for a quick sale.

BRRRR — The BRRRR strategy was coined by Brandon Turner and stands for Buy, Rehab, Rent, Refinance, Repeat. This strategy is where an investor buys a fixer-upper property using short-term funds (oftentimes cash, hard money, private money, or other creative means), fixes up the property, rents out the newly renovated property, and seeks a new long-term loan (a refinance) to pay off the old short-term loan. This refinance will free up the short-term capital that was used, allowing the investor to repeat the process again and again. For more information, check out the book "Buy, Rehab, Rent, Refinance, Repeat" by David Greene.

Buy and Hold — The buy and hold strategy is long-term investing when a real estate investor purchases a property with the intention of holding onto and renting it for the foreseeable future.

Buyer's Agent — A buying agent, or a purchasing agent, is an agent who works with buyers to find and purchase a property. The buying agent works for a commission that is typically paid by the seller at closing.

C

Capital Expenditure — Capital expenditure or CapEx refers to large expenses that are performed infrequently but should still be budgeted for.

Examples include a new roof or systems like a furnace or air conditioning unit.

Capital Gains Tax — When you sell an asset for more than you paid for it, you trigger what is called a capital gains tax.

Capital Improvement — Capital improvement is the addition of permanent structural changes to a property that add to the property value or adapt the property to new uses.

Capitalization Rate aka "Cap Rate" — The capitalization rate or cap rate is used in the world of real estate investing to indicate the rate of return that an investor can expect on any given real estate investment property. This is measured by a formula based on the net income that the property is expected to produce and is calculated by dividing net operating income by the property asset value and is expressed as a percentage. This calculation is typically used by real estate investors to understand the potential ROI on an investment property. While it is a useful calculation, this should not be the only deciding factor when considering an investment property. The capitalization rate indicates the property's intrinsic, natural, and un-leveraged rate of return.

Cash Flow — In real estate terms, cash flow is the byproduct of owning a rental property and leasing it to tenants for a monthly rental income. To elaborate on this, real estate investors look for rental properties reaping positive cash flow returns or, in other words, they invest in positive cash flow properties.

Cash On Cash Return (COCR or CRR) — A cash-on-cash return is a rate of return often used in real estate transactions that calculates the cash income earned on the cash invested in a property.

Cash-Out Refinance — A cash-out refinance will replace a person's existing mortgage with a new home loan for more than is currently owed on a property. The difference is refunded to the property owner in cash and can be spent on home improvements, debt consolidation, or any other financial needs. In order to use a cash-out refinance, a property owner would need to have built up equity in the property.

Cash Reserves — Cash reserves refer to the money an individual has set aside for unexpected expenses like home improvement emergencies, such as plumbing issues, appliance replacements, flooding, etc., as well as vacancies, capital expenditures, and non-paying tenants.

Certificate of Title — This is the state-issued document that identifies the owner of real property. A certificate of title provides documentary evidence of the right of ownership so that the seller is actually able to transfer title and sell a property.

Certified Commercial Investment Member (CCIM) — A CCIM (Certified Commercial Investment Member) is a recognized expert in the commercial and investment real estate industry. The designation process ensures that CCIMs are proficient not only in theory but also in practice.

Chain of Title — This is the sequence of historical transfers of a title of real property from sellers to buyers. This is a valuable tool to identify the past owners of any given property. This chain will follow the title from the original owners to the current owners.

Clear Title — A clear title is a title that is clear of any type of lien or anything else that might pose a question about legal ownership. An owner with a clear title has legal ownership of the title and property and can transfer this title legally to a purchaser.

Closing — The closing is when the buyer and seller sign the official papers to transfer ownership.

Closing Costs — This is any cost that is associated with the purchase of a property that is due at closing. This typically includes the down payment on the property and any other fees associated with purchasing a home, such as title insurance, taxes, lender costs, and some upfront housing expenses.

Cloud on Title — This is a document, claim, or unreleased lien that might invalidate or make it difficult to transfer a title. Cloud on title is usually discovered during the title search once a property is under contract.

Co-Borrower — A co-borrower is the second person on a mortgage loan. This can be anyone from a parent or friend to a significant other or spouse. Co-borrowers are used to help qualify for a loan and are also equally responsible for the mortgage should the initial borrower default.

Commercial Real Estate (CRE) — A commercial property refers to a real estate property that is used for business purposes or large-scale residential dwellings, such as apartment buildings.

Comparative Market Analysis (CMA) — This is an examination of the prices of different properties within the same area as the property a buyer is considering for purchase. Real estate agents perform this analysis to determine an accurate listing price.

Consumer Price Index — The Consumer Price Index indicates how much prices of consumer goods and services have increased over a set period of time.

Contingency Clause — A contingency clause is a portion of a contract that will require certain things to take place before the contract can be considered valid. This often is a part of a conditional offer made on a property during a real estate transaction.

Contract For Deed — A Contract for Deed is a tool that can allow buyers who either do not qualify for traditional lending options or want a faster financing option to purchase property.

Co-Tenancy Clause — A co-tenancy clause in retail lease contracts allows tenants to reduce their rent if key tenants or a certain number of tenants leave the retail space.

Covenants, Conditions, & Restrictions — Commonly called CC&R, these are a set of rules established by a developer or homeowners association that govern residences in a particular neighborhood or condominium.

CC&R may put restrictions on parking, paint colors, noise-levels, and pets, for example.

Curb Appeal — This term is often used to describe the appeal of a property for sale when the property is viewed from the street.

D

Debt Service Coverage Ratio (DSCR) — The debt service coverage ratio (DSCR), also known as "debt coverage ratio" (DCR), is the ratio of operating income available to debt servicing for interest, principal, and lease payments.

Debt-to-Income Ratio (DTI) — A buyer's debt-to-income ratio compares how much a buyer owes monthly versus how much they earn monthly. This ratio is used during the underwriting process of escrow to determine how much house you can afford as a buyer. More specifically, it is the percentage of gross monthly income that goes toward payments for rent, mortgages, credit cards, car payments, or any other debt the buyer possesses.

Deed — A deed is a legal document that passes and confirms an interest, right, or property and is signed, attested, delivered, and sealed. It is commonly associated with transferring the title of a property from the seller to the buyer.

Deed Book — Deed books can be found at the county courthouse and are under the jurisdiction of the registrar of deeds. The deed book contains the record of property transfers.

Deed of Trust (DOT) — A Deed of Trust is a type of secured real-estate transaction that some states use instead of mortgages. A deed of trust involves three parties: a lender, a borrower, and a trustee. The lender gives the borrower money. In exchange, the borrower gives the lender one or more promissory notes.

Default Within Real Estate — A default is when a property owner fails to make monthly mortgage payments and therefore defaults on their mortgage loan. When the mortgage payments are not made and a borrower default on the loan, the property can then be taken away by the lender through a process called foreclosure.

Deficiency Balance — This is the amount of the loan that remains unpaid after the lender has taken the property back from the owner.

Delinquent — This term is typically used when a borrower is late or overdue on a mortgage payment.

Depreciation — Is when a property decreases in value.

Downturns — When the economy or real estate market has softened, resulting in properties typically taking longer to sell.

Dual Agency — Dual agency is when a real estate agent represents both the buyer and the seller in a single transaction.

Due On Sale Clause (DOS) — A due-on-sale clause is a clause in a loan or promissory note that stipulates that the full balance of the loan may be called due (repaid in full) upon sale or transfer of ownership of the property used to secure the note. The lender has the right, but not the obligation, to call the note due in such a circumstance.

E

Earnest Money — After an offer is accepted, a deposit is made to the seller by the buyer as a symbol of good faith that you will be following through on buying the property. This deposit can be forfeited if the buyer does not follow through on the purchase.

Easement — Is the legal right to use someone else's land for a specific and limited purpose. When someone is granted an easement, they are legally allowed to use the property, but the property title and ownership remain in the possession of the owner.

Effective Gross Income — Effective gross income, or EGI, can be calculated by taking the potential gross income from an investment property, adding other forms of income generated by that property, and subtracting vacancy and collection losses.

Egress — When buying a property, there are certain things that qualify a room as "conforming" or "non-conforming." For example, a basement room with regular windows would be considered a "non-conforming" bedroom. Egress is a way to exit the property, and in order for a room to be a legal bedroom, it must have two points of egress or exit.

Ejectment — This is a common law term for the civil action to recover the possession of a title to the land.

Eminent Domain — Refers to the right of the government to take private property and convert it to public use.

Equity — Is the difference between the market value of a property and the amount of money that is still owed on the loan. Equity can accrue naturally through the market or can be forced into the home based on improvements made by the owner.

Equity Stripping — Is a set of strategies designed to reduce overall equity in a property. These can be used by debtors as means of making properties unattractive to creditors.

Escrow Agent — An escrow agent is the person that holds property in trust for third parties while a transaction is finalized on the property in question.

Escrow Agreement — This is the contract that defines an arrangement between parties where one-party deposits an asset with a third party. This third party then delivers the asset to the second party when the conditions of the contract are met.

Estate — A word with deep legal origins, "estate" has been consistently defined for centuries while adapting to the needs of the times. In essence, one's estate is everything they own; it is everything that belongs to a person.

Eviction — The legal method for removing a tenant from a rental property. Eviction typically takes place after the tenant fails to make their monthly rent payments on time.

F

Fair Housing Act — The Fair Housing Act was initiated to make sure that everyone who applies for housing has the right to be treated the same. For landlords, this means you cannot discriminate against potential tenants based on color, disability, familial status, national origin, race, religion, or sex.

Fair Market Rent (FMR) — Fair market rent is the monthly rent a particular property type is likely to receive.

Fair Market Value (FMV) — This is an estimate of the market value of a property. At its simplest, it is the price that a property would sell for in a fair and open market.

Federal Housing Administration — The Federal Housing Administration, generally known as "FHA," provides mortgage insurance on loans made by FHA-approved lenders throughout the United States and its territories.

Fee Simple — A fee simple represents absolute ownership of land; therefore, the owner may do whatever he or she chooses with the land.

FHA Loan — This is a type of mortgage loan that is insured by the Federal Housing Administration. These types of loans are popular among first-time home buyers due to the low-down payment requirements — as low as 3.5% — as well as a more lenient credit score requirement.

First Mortgage — This is the first mortgage loan on a property and has priority over all other liens or claims on a property in the event of a default on the home.

Fix and Flip — This term is coined for properties that need a lot of rehabilitation to make them appealing to buyers. Real estate investors will buy the property, renovate it, and resell the property for a profit.

Fixed Price Purchase Option — A fixed price purchase option is the right, but not the obligation, to buy a leased property at the end of a lease term at a price determined from the onset of the lease agreement.

Fixed Rate Mortgage — This is a fully amortizing mortgage loan where the interest rate on the note remains the same through the term of the loan.

Forced Equity — Is equity that is instantly put into the home by making improvements to it. By improving the home, you not only increase the home's market value but also increase the market rent, which permits you to make more money each month and pay off your property faster. This is the best way to build equity in a home versus waiting for the home's market value to increase naturally.

Foreclosure — Is the legal process in which a lender or bank takes control of a property, evicts the homeowner, and sells the home after a homeowner is unable to make full principal and interest payments on his or her mortgage, as decided upon in the mortgage contract.

For Sale by Owner (FSBO) — For sale by owner is a process by which a homeowner sells their home directly instead of going through a brokerage firm to sell the property. The benefit to the seller is that there is no commission to pay out at the end of the selling process.

Fractional Ownership — Fractional ownership is a method in which several unrelated parties can share in, and mitigate the risk of, ownership of a real estate property.

Freddie Mac Federal Home Loan Mortgage Corporation (Freddie Mac) — A private corporation founded by Congress, the Federal Home Loan Mortgage Corporation's mission is to promote stability and affordability in the housing market by purchasing mortgages from banks and other loan makers.

G

Gentrification — Is a process where a neighborhood undergoes urban development, involving an influx of higher-income residents to an otherwise abandoned or rundown area. Gentrification is a controversial political and social topic.

Gift of Equity — The gift of equity is when a family member sells you a property for below market value. This difference is considered an amount of equity. This equity can be used toward the down payment or to help pay off debt in order to qualify to buy the home.

Ginnie Mae (GNMA) — The Government National Mortgage Association (commonly referred to as Ginnie Mae is a U.S. government corporation that guarantees the timely payment of principal and interest on mortgage-backed securities (MBSs) issued by approved Ginnie Mae lenders.

Graduated Lease — Refers to an agreement under which a tenant and landlord agree to a periodic adjustment of monthly payments. This typically occurs when the market conditions increase, and the landlord then needs to increase the price on the lease.

Gross Rent Multiplier (GRM) — Is the ratio of the price of a real estate investment to its annual rental income before accounting for expenses such as property taxes, insurance, and utilities. GRM is the number of years the property would take to pay for itself in gross received rent. For a prospective real estate investor, a lower GRM represents a better opportunity.

Ground Lease — A ground lease refers to an agreement between a tenant and a property owner that allows the tenant to develop a piece of property during the lease period. After the lease, all of these developments are to be transferred over to the property owner.

H

Hard Money Lender (HML) — A hard money lender is a private lender that uses property collateral instead of credit scores in order to qualify lending a buyer money.

Hard Money Loan — Is a way to borrow without using traditional mortgage lenders. Loans come from individuals or investors who lend money based (for the most part) on the property you are using as collateral and not based off credit scores. When loans need to happen quickly, or when traditional lenders will not approve a loan, hard money may be the only option.

Hazard Insurance — Protects a homeowner against the costs of damage from fire, vandalism, smoke, and other causes. When you take out a mortgage, the lender will require you to take out hazard insurance to protect their investment. Many lenders will incorporate the insurance payment into your monthly mortgage payment.

Home Equity Line of Credit (HELOC) — Is when a property owner borrows money against the equity that has been built up in said property.

Holding Costs — When real estate investors purchase property, their main goal is to sell the property for a profit, but during this process, the investor must take into consideration the amount of money they will need to pay out before the investment is re-sold. Holding costs are also known as carrying costs. When calculating the holding costs, investors must include the purchase price and deduct operating income to come to an estimated figure.

Home Appraisal — Real estate appraisal, property valuation, or land valuation is the process of developing an opinion of value for real property. Real estate transactions often require appraisals because they occur infrequently and every property is unique, unlike corporate stocks, which are traded daily and are identical.

Home Equity — This is the current market value of your home, minus what a borrower still owes on a mortgage.

Home Equity Loan — A home equity loan is a type of loan in which the borrower uses the equity of his or her home as collateral.

Home Inspection — A home inspection is something that a home buyer will pay to have conducted during the escrow period. A home inspector will come to the property and look at different aspects of the home that may deter a buyer from wanting to follow through with the purchase.

Homeowners Association (HOA) — The primary purpose of a home-owner's association is to manage a large property's or neighborhood's common areas, such as roads, parks, and pools. Homeowners are obligated to pay dues, which can be anything from $100 to $10,000 a year, depending on the building/neighborhood and its amenities. This is an added monthly expense on top of a mortgage payment and should be considered as such when home buying.

Home Warranty — A home warranty is an annual service contract that covers the repair or replacement of important appliances and systems' components in the event they break down.

House Hacking — Is a strategy in which the property owner lives within the investment property and lives for free (or almost free) based on other tenants paying rent that covers the whole mortgage. This strategy is typically done with a multifamily unit but can also be done in single family homes by renting out extra rooms.

Housing Starts — Is the number of new projects for residential construction that began over the duration of any given month and is a pivotal economic indicator.

I

Individual Retirement Account (IRA) — An IRA is an account set up at a financial institution that allows an individual to save for retirement with tax-free growth or on a tax-deferred basis.

Inflation — In simple terms, inflation is a quantitative measure of the rate at which the average price level of a basket of selected goods and services in an economy increases over a period of time.

Ingress — The right to enter a property.

Interest Within Real Estate — Interest can be defined as the cost of borrowing money and is usually expressed as a yearly percentage that is paid as part of your monthly loan payment.

Interest Only Loan (I/O) — An interest-only loan is a loan in which the borrower pays only the interest for some or all of the term, with the principal balance unchanged during the interest-only period.

Interim Interest Mortgage — Refers to the interest that accrues on your mortgage between the closing date and the date of record. This is the time between when you close on the mortgage and the end of the month.

Internal Rate of Return (IRR) — The internal rate of return is a measure of an investment's rate of return.

Intestate — Refers to when a person dies before determining a will. An intestate estate is also one in which the will presented to the court was deemed to be invalid.

J

Joint Tenancy — The holding of an estate or property jointly by two or more parties, the share of each passing to the other or others on death.

Joint Tenants In Estate Law — Joint tenancy is a special form of ownership by two or more persons of the same property. The individuals, who are called joint tenants, share equal ownership of the property and have the equal, undivided right to keep or dispose of the property.

Joint Venture (JV) — A commercial enterprise undertaken jointly by two or more parties which otherwise retain their distinct identities.

Judicial Foreclosure — Refers to foreclosure cases that go through the court system.

Jumbo Loan — A jumbo loan is a type of mortgage that is used to finance real estate that is too expensive for a conventional conforming loan.

L

Landlord — A person or company who owns property that they allow other people to live in, in exchange for monthly rent.

Land Trust — A land trust is a legal entity that takes ownership of, or authority over, a piece of property at the behest of the property owner.

Land Value — Is the value of a piece of property, including both the value of the land itself as well as any improvements that have been made to the property over time.

Lease — The legally binding contract that governs the circumstances in which a landlord will rent their property to a tenant.

Lease Option (L/O) — A lease option is an agreement that gives a renter a choice to purchase the rented property during or at the end of the rental period.

Lenders — Are people or companies that allow you to borrow money with the promise that it will be repaid. Repayment includes principal and interest and may include monthly payments or a lump sum payment.

Lessee — A lessee is a person who rents land or property from a lessor. The lessee is also known as the "tenant" and must uphold specific obligations as defined in the lease agreement and by law.

Lessor — The lessor is the property owner or landlord that rents out the property to the lessee.

Leverage — Is the use of various financial instruments or borrowed capital — in other words, debt — to increase the potential return of an investment. It is commonly used when talking about the real estate market.

Lien — A legal interest in a property, which must be paid in full before the property can be sold. If there is a lien on a property, this is typically identified in the escrow process and will break the contract.

Lien Waiver — In the mechanics lien process, a lien waiver is a document from a contractor, subcontractor, materials supplier, equipment lessor, or other party to the construction project stating they have received payment and waive any future lien rights to the property for the amount paid.

Line of Credit (LOC) — A line of credit is a preset amount of money that a bank or credit union has agreed to lend you. You can draw from the line of credit when you need it, up to the maximum amount. You'll pay interest on the amount you borrow.

Listing — A listing is what a property for sale is often referred to as by a real estate broker or agent.

List Price — The price at which a property is listed by the seller.

Live-in Flip — This is when a property purchaser lives in the property as they flip in order to limit costs during the time of the flip.

Loan Estimate — A loan estimate is a three-page form that a potential borrower receives after applying for a mortgage. The loan estimate tells the borrower important details about the loan requested. The form provides important information, including the estimated interest rate, monthly payment, and total closing costs for the loan.

Loan Policy — A loan policy protects the lender's interests and is based on the dollar amount someone is borrowing from the bank, not on the full value of the property.

Loan-To-Value (LTV) — The loan-to-value (LTV) ratio is a financial term used by lenders to express the ratio of a loan to the value of an asset purchased.

M

Market Value — Is the price an asset would fetch in the marketplace.

Maximum Allowable Offer (MAO) — Is the maximum price point at which investors in a real estate deal can realistically expect to pull in a profit while minimizing the risk of losing money.

Mortgage — A mortgage is a legal agreement by which a bank or other creditor lends money at interest in exchange for taking title of the debtor's property, with the condition that the conveyance of title becomes void upon the payment of the debt.

Mortgage Broker — These are mortgage experts who provide different lenders, loan types, and rates for buyers without upfront charges.

Multi-Family — A building or structure that is designed to house several different families in separate housing units.

Multiple Listing Service (MLS) — A multiple listing service is a service used by a group of real estate brokers. Once a buyer begins working with a real estate agent/broker, they will typically be set up with an MLS email drip that will send new listings every day.

N

National Housing Act — The American Housing Act of 1949 was a sweeping expansion of the federal role in mortgage insurance and issuance and the construction of public housing.

Negative Equity — Occurs when the value of real estate property falls below the outstanding balance on the mortgage used to purchase that property.

Negative Equity — Is calculated by taking the current market value of the property and subtracting the balance on the outstanding mortgage.

Net Operating Income (NOI) — Is a calculation used to analyze the profitability of income-generating real estate investments. NOI equals all revenue from the property, minus all reasonably necessary operating expenses.

Net Worth — Financial resources or other wealth belonging to a particular person, especially when used for investment purposes.

No-Appraisal Refinancing — A no-appraisal mortgage is a type of home loan refinancing for which the lender does not require an appraisal, meaning an independent opinion of the property's current fair market value is not necessary.

Note Mortgage Notes — Are a written promise to repay a specified sum of money plus interest at a specified rate and length of time to fulfill the promise.

O

Offer — An offer is when a buyer puts in a price offer on a home that the seller can accept or counter.

Open House — An open house is held by the selling agent in order for prospective buyers to come and look at a property. It enables interested parties to view property without scheduling a showing with their agent.

Open Listing — An open listing is a non-exclusive real estate contract in which more than one broker may be employed to sell a property, including the owners themselves.

Owner Occupied (OO) — Owner-occupancy or homeownership is a form of housing tenure where a person, called the owner-occupier, owner-occupant, or homeowner, owns the home in which they live.

P

Personal Use Property — Is a type of property that an individual does not use for business purposes or as an investment.

Pocket Listing — A pocket listing is a signed real estate listing that is not entered into the multiple listing service (MLS).

Power of Sale Clause — Is a clause written into a mortgage note authorizing the mortgagee to sell the property in the event of default in order to repay the mortgage debt.

Pre-Approval Letter — A pre-approval letter is a document that states the loan amount a lender is willing to extend to a borrower. It is not a guarantee to lend, but it carries significant weight, especially to other parties in a real estate transaction, such as agents and sellers.

Private Mortgage Insurance or (PMI) — Is a type of mortgage insurance a buyer might be required to have if he or she uses anything other than a conventional loan. Like other kinds of mortgage insurance, PMI protects the lender if the buyer stops making monthly loan payments.

Probate — Is the legal process through which a deceased person's estate is properly distributed to heirs and designated beneficiaries and any debt owed to creditors is paid off.

Proof of Funds — Is a document that stipulates that a buyer is financially capable of securing a mortgage or has the funds necessary to make an all-cash purchase in a real estate transaction.

Property Manager — Is an individual or a company that is hired by a property owner in order to run the rental property. Typically, property owners will hire a property management company to run it day to day because they are unwilling or do not have the time to do so.

Q

Quiet Title — A quiet title action is a circuit court action, or lawsuit, intended to establish or settle the title to a property, especially when there is a disagreement. It is a lawsuit brought to remove a claim or objection on a title.

Quitclaim Deed — Are most often used to transfer property within a family. For example, when an owner gets married and wants to add a spouse's name to the title or when the owners divorce and one spouse's name is removed from the title.

R

Repair Costs — Repair costs within real estate investing are typically applied to fix and flips or even BRRR properties where there are repairs and renovations to be done. Repair costs should be properly calculated before buying any investment property in order to accurately assess a deal.

Real Estate — Refers to property containing land, buildings, or both.

Real Estate Agents — Are licensed professionals who arrange real estate transactions for either a buyer or a seller.

Real Estate Brokers — Are real estate agents but with a broker's license. They work for a real estate brokerage and assist buyers or sellers in the transfer of ownership of a property, much like a real estate agent.

Real Estate Owned (REO) — Is the name given to foreclosed-upon real estate. This happens when a borrower fails to make monthly mortgage payments and therefore defaults on the loan. In this case, the property goes back to the bank or lender for sale. It is typically sold at a discounted price.

Realtor — A person who acts as an agent for the sale and purchase of buildings and land. Also known as a real estate agent.

Recession — A period of temporary economic decline during which trade and industrial activity are reduced, generally identified by a fall in GDP in two successive quarters.

Refinance Rate — One of the best reasons to refinance is to lower the interest rate on your existing loan. Historically, the rule of thumb is that refinancing is a good idea if you can reduce your interest rate by at least 2%. However, many lenders say 1% savings is enough of an incentive to refinance.

Refinancing — Is done to allow a borrower to obtain a better interest term and rate. The first loan is paid off, allowing the second loan to be created, instead of simply making a new mortgage and throwing out the original mortgage.

Real Estate Investment Trust (REIT) — Essentially, REITs are corporations that own and manage a portfolio of real estate properties and mortgages.

Rent-To-Own Homes (RTO) — Is when a tenant signs a rental agreement or lease that has an option to buy the house or condo later, usually within three years. The renter's monthly payments will include rent payments and additional payments that will go toward a down payment for purchasing the home.

Reserve Fund — Is a savings account or other highly liquid asset set aside by an individual or business to meet any future costs or financial obligations, especially those arising unexpectedly.

Residential Rental Property — Is a type of rented real property, such as a house or apartment complex.

Return On Investment (ROI) — Return on investment measures how much money or net profit is made on an investment, displayed as a percentage of the cost of that investment.

Reverse Exchange — A reverse 1031 exchange is a tax deferment strategy that allows real estate investors to purchase a second investment property before selling their relinquished investment property and, importantly, defer capital gains taxes and other taxes that you would normally need to pay upon sale of a property.

Reverse Mortgage — A financial agreement in which a homeowner relinquishes equity in their home in exchange for regular payments, typically to supplement retirement income.

Rural Housing Service USDAs — Are multifamily housing programs that offer loans to provide affordable rental housing for very low-, low-, and moderate-income residents, the elderly, and persons with disabilities.

S

Sales and Purchase Agreement — A sales and purchase agreement (SPA) is a legal contract that obligates a buyer to buy and a seller to sell a product or service. SPAs are found in all types of businesses but are most often associated with real estate deals as a way of finalizing the interests of both parties before closing the deal.

Security Deposit — Is a paid amount of money to the landlord meant to ensure that rent will be paid, and other responsibilities of the lease performed (e.g., paying for damage caused by the tenant). The laws surrounding these deposits vary from state to state.

Seller-Financed Sale — Is a loan provided by the seller of a property or business to the purchaser.

Seller-Paid Points (or seller contributions) — Are lump sum payments (or finance charges) made by the seller to the buyer's lender to reduce the cost of the loan to the buyer.

Shared Equity Finance Agreements — A shared equity finance agreement is a financial agreement entered into by two parties who would like to purchase a piece of real estate together.

Short Refinance — Is a transaction in which a lender agrees to refinance a borrower's home for the current market value, in effect making it more cost effective for the borrower.

Short Sale — A short sale is a sale of real estate in which the net proceeds from selling the property will fall short of the debts secured by liens against the property.

Squatter — A person who unlawfully occupies an uninhabited building or unused land.

Sublease Lease from One Tenant (lessee) to Another (called subtenant or sublessee) — The agreement between the landlord (the lessor) and the first lessee remains in force and governs the terms of the sublease.

Syndicate — A syndicate is a temporary, professional financial services alliance formed for the purpose of handling a large transaction that would be hard or impossible for the entities involved to handle individually.

Syndications — A Real estate syndication is an effective way for investors to pool their financial and intellectual resources to invest in properties and projects much bigger than they could afford or manage on their own.

T

Tax Lien — A tax lien is the government's claim on your property and is generally placed when a taxpayer, such as a business or individual, fails to pay taxes owed.

Tenancy In Common — Tenancy in common is a specific type of concurrent, or simultaneous, ownership of real property by two or more parties. All tenants in common hold an individual, undivided ownership interest in the property. This means that each party has the right to alienate or transfer their ownership interest.

Tenants By Entirety (TBE) — Is a method in some states by which married couples can hold the title to a property. In order for one spouse to modify his or her interest in the property in any way, the consent of both spouses is required by tenants by entirety.

Tenement or Tenement House — Is a run-down and often overcrowded apartment house, especially in a poor section of a large city. By law, any species of permanent property, as lands, houses, rents, an office, or a franchise, that may be held of another.

Timeshare (sometimes called vacation ownership) — Is a property with a divided form of ownership or use rights. These properties are typically resort condominium units, in which 26 multiple parties hold rights to use the property, and each owner of the same accommodation is allotted a period of time.

Title — In property law, a title is a bundle of rights in a piece of property in which a party may own either a legal interest or equitable interest.

Title Commitment — A title commitment (or whatever name yours goes by) is basically the title company's promise to issue a title insurance policy for the property after closing. The title commitment contains the same terms, conditions, and exclusions that will be in the actual insurance policy.

Title Defect — A title defect refers to any potential threat to the current owner's full right or claim to sell a property. The property has a publicly recorded issue, like a lien, mortgage, or judgment, that gives another party a claim to the property.

Title Insurance — Every title insurance policy covers either a homeowner or the lender that financed the mortgage for the property. Lenders require you to pay for lender's title insurance as part of your mortgage closing costs. Homeowner's title insurance is mostly optional and is paid for by the seller or the buyer of the property.

Title Search — A title search is done to verify the seller's right to transfer ownership. It is used to discover any claims, errors, assessments, debts, or other restrictions on the property.

Triple Net Lease (NNN) — A triple net lease (triple-Net or NNN) is a lease agreement on a property whereby the tenant or lessee promises to pay all the expenses of the property including real estate taxes, building insurance, and maintenance.

Truth in Lending — The Truth in Lending Act (TILA) is a federal law passed in 1968 to ensure that consumers are treated fairly by businesses in the lending marketplace and are informed about the true cost of credit.

Turnkey Property — Is a fully renovated home or apartment building that an investor can purchase and immediately rent out.

U

Under Contract — Means that a buyer's offer has been accepted by the seller.

Underwriting — Underwriting is when an individual or business entity seeks funding for a real estate project or purchase and the loan request is scrutinized to determine how much risk the lender is willing to accept. This procedure is performed by an underwriter.

Unsecured Loan — An unsecured loan is a loan that is issued and supported only by the borrower's creditworthiness, rather than by any type of collateral.

Use and Occupancy(U&O) — Refers to a type of permit required by some local governments whenever real property is transferred.

V

Vacancy Rate — Is the ratio of rental units not rented versus the total number in the building.

Voluntary Foreclosure — A voluntary foreclosure is a foreclosure proceeding that is initiated by a borrower who is unable to continue making loan payments on a property to avoid further payments and prevent involuntary foreclosure and eviction.

W

Waiver — A waiver is the voluntary action of a person or party that removes that person's or party's right or particular ability in an agreement.

Warranty Deed — A warranty deed is one in which a property owner, when transferring the title, warrants that he or she owns the property free and clear of all liens. A warranty deed is used in most property sales. The warranty deed says that: The grantor is the rightful owner and has the right to transfer the title.

Warranty of Title — A warranty of title is a guarantee by a seller to a buyer that the seller has the right to transfer ownership and no one else has rights to the property.

Workout Agreement — A workout agreement is a mutual agreement between a lender and borrower to renegotiate terms on a loan that is in default. Generally, the workout includes waiving any existing defaults and restructuring the loan's terms and covenants.

#

1031 Exchange — The IRS code's Section 1031 makes it possible for a real estate investor to defer payment of capital gains taxes on an investment property upon its sale, as long as another "like kind" property is bought with the profit from the sale of the investment property.

Bonus Materials

Unlock Your Potential with the Real Estate Investing Readiness Assessment

You've just taken a significant step by reading **The Real Estate Wealth Creator Blueprint** which is packed with insights and strategies for building wealth through real estate. But before you dive deeper into the world of real estate investing, it's essential to assess whether you're truly ready to embark on this journey.

Why you need to take the Real Estate Investing Readiness Assessment

- Imagine the feeling of financial freedom, the security of passive income, and the pride of owning properties that grow in value over time. Real estate can change your life — but only if you're prepared to seize the opportunities it offers.

- Real estate investing requires more than just enthusiasm. It demands a clear understanding of your strengths, resources, and the areas where you may need to grow. The Real Estate Investing Readiness Assessment provides you with a roadmap to evaluate your preparedness.

- The real estate market is dynamic, and opportunities come and go. Don't let uncertainty or lack of readiness hold you back. Assess your readiness now and make informed decisions that can fast-track your path to wealth.

Take Action Today!

Start by taking our Real Estate Investing Readiness Assessment. This short and comprehensive tool will help you understand where you stand and what steps you need to take to succeed in real estate investing.

How to Access the Real Estate Investor Readiness Assessment:

- **Visit: https://dexter-b-qwkihs3i.scoreapp.com/**

- **Or scan the QR code below**

How to Develop Your Courage

Courage is one of those intangible forces that guarantee success in business and in life. It is my strongest belief that courage is like a muscle, in that it can be developed or enlarged. Ask yourself this question: What could I accomplish if I were a more courageous person? This piece will expose you to some concepts that will undoubtedly help you develop your courage.

Defining Courage: Courage is the willingness to confront fears, doubts, and insecurities in order to accomplish a particular task.

In examining our definition closely, I want to draw your attention to the word confront. Any time we confront fears, doubts, and insecurities, our courage muscle grows bigger and stronger.

If confronting fears, doubts, and insecurities is the key to developing our courage, the question becomes, "What causes an individual to confront the destructive forces listed above?"

I believe the answer is this: When we come to certain realizations in our lives, these realizations serve as major wake-up calls empowering us to confront any fear, doubt, or insecurity.

5 Powerful Realizations That Will Help Develop Your Courage

I have listed 5 powerful realizations. This is not an all-inclusive list, but it will get you started on the road to being more courageous. □

1. Realize God is with you — when God is with you, there is access to His presence, power, protection, and provision.

2. Realize that courage grows and fear dissipates as you take action.

3. Realize that courage grows as you connect with like-minded others. You can borrow the courage of others.

4. Realize that you have confronted things in your past and defeated them.

5. Realize that victory is already yours and that you are merely walking it out on a daily basis.

If you grab hold of those 5 Powerful Realizations, you will become a courageous person and accomplish magnificent things both in business and in life.

For more educational materials like this please visit *DexterBJenkins.com*.

Recommended Real Estate Investing Educational Resources

- Strategic Real Estate Investing by Billy Epperhart
- The Peebles Path to Real Estate Wealth by Don Peebles
- More Leads, More Deals, More Profits by Mark Lane
- The Millionaire Real Estate Investor by Gary Keller
- The Book on Negotiating Real Estate by J Scott, Mark Ferguson, & Carol Scott
- Barron's Dictionary of Real Estate Terms
- Every Landlord's Tax Deduction Guide | *Nolo.com*
- Bigger Pockets | BiggerPockets.com

The 10 Commandments of Real Estate Investing

God gave Moses 10 commandments for the children of Israel to live by that would guarantee their success as they journeyed through the desert to the promise land. I have listed my top 10 real estate investing commandments that will be of great benefit to you as you embark on your real estate investing journey. You will also find some bonus commandments as it was hard to stop at 10.

1. Thou shalt not fail to get started: The failure to get started is the only investing mistake you cannot overcome.

2. Thou shalt not go it alone: You must build a team of attorneys, realtors, tradespeople, etc.

3. Thou shalt always maintain consistent deal flow.

4. Thou shalt not overpay on the front end as profits are made at the buy and realized on the sale.

5. Thou shalt not have only one exit or monetization strategy.

6. Thou shall not speculate when analyzing deals: The numbers are the numbers!

7. Thou shalt always have a multitude of banking and money relationships.

8. Thou shalt master the 4 real estate investing wealth generators of cash flow, appreciation, tax benefits, and debt paydown.

9. Thou shalt not take the word of a seller: Do your due diligence.

10. Thou shalt not be afraid to invest in your education (paid and

unpaid).

11. Thou shalt always be networking as business takes place through relationships.

12. Thou shalt always cash flow.

13. Thou shalt always have cash reserves.

14. Thou shalt always properly screen your tenants (credit checks, eviction courts, references, etc.).

15. Thou shalt not bow down to fear: Do it anyway.

16. Thou shalt not be afraid to walk away from a potential deal.

17. Thou shall not succumb to paralysis of analysis.

18. Thou shalt always be looking out for quality tradespeople.

19. Thou shalt always treat your people with respect.

20. Thou shalt not compare yourself to others: Everyone has different goals and aspirations; just run your race.

For more educational materials like this, please visit *DexterBJenkins.com*.

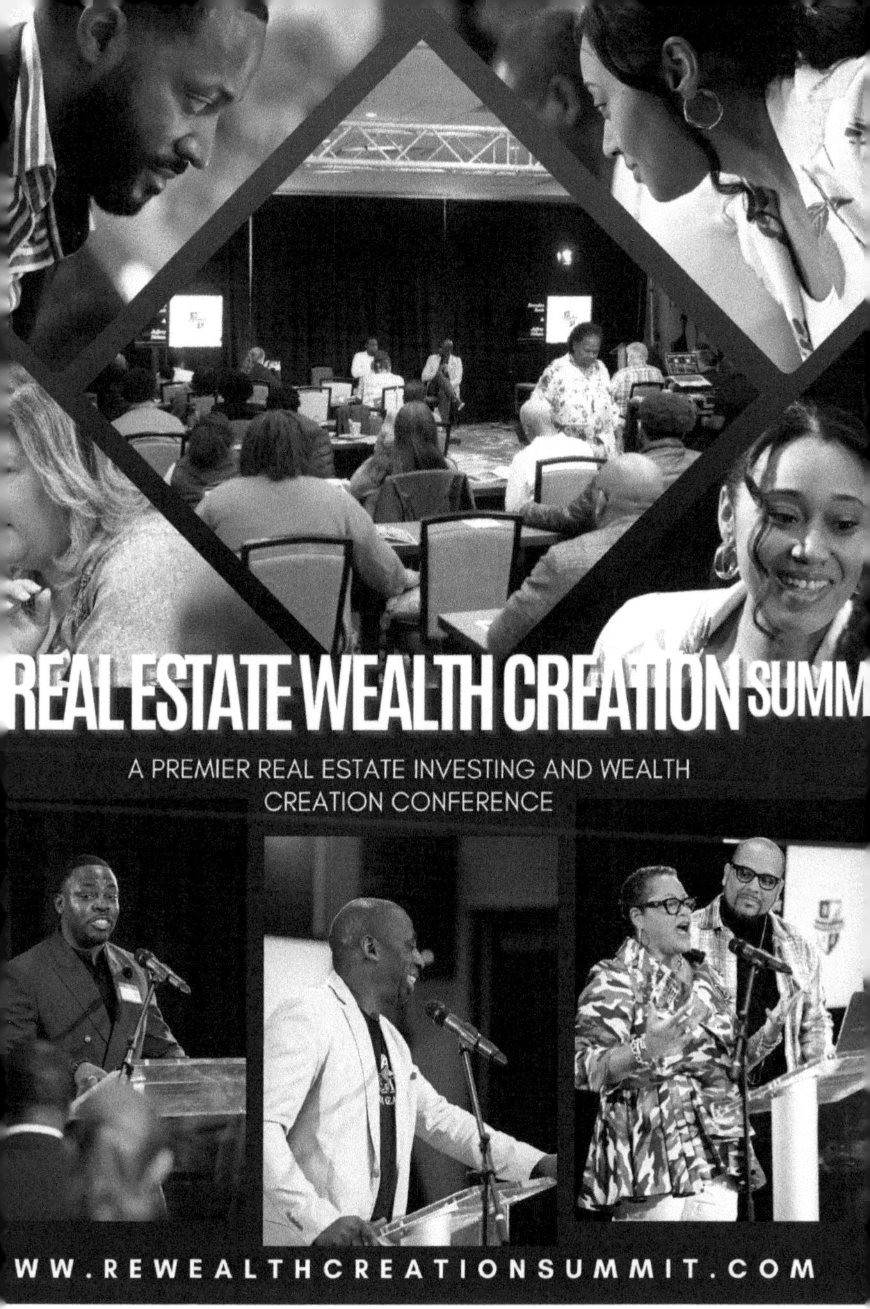
REAL ESTATE WEALTH CREATION SUMM
A PREMIER REAL ESTATE INVESTING AND WEALTH CREATION CONFERENCE
WW.REWEALTHCREATIONSUMMIT.COM

RAISING YOUR
FINANCIAL
INTELLIGENCE
Q4 202
ISSUE NO. 0
$27
THE
ULTIMATE
WEALTH
BUILDING
HACK
Asset Accumulation
HOW-TO HARNESS
THE POWER OF
COMPOUND INTEREST
A powerful Financial Ally
IMPROVED FINANCES
Two Critical Questions to Ask
for Improved Finances
PUBLISHED BY DEXTERBJENKINS.COM

WEALTH
CONVERSATIO
MONEY SESSIO
Need clarity, advice, or strateg
$997
I offer practical, simple, easy
implement, money solutions,
well as my personal "how to'
for 60 minutes at a time.
SCAN
ME
BOOK NO
www.dexterbjenkins.com

www.ingramcontent.com/pod-product-compliance
Lightning Source LLC
LaVergne TN
LVHW050917210926
848482LV00012B/472
9798991010399